Freelancing

A Beginner's Guide on Freelance and Remote Work

(How to Make Part-time Side Income Through Social Media)

Helen Talbert

Published By **Jackson Denver**

Helen Talbert

Freelancing: A Beginner's Guide on Freelance and Remote Work (How to Make Part-time Side Income Through Social Media)

ISBN 978-1-77485-613-0

No part of this guidebook shall be reproduced in any form without permission in writing from the publisher except in the case of brief quotations embodied in critical articles or reviews.

Legal & Disclaimer

The information contained in this ebook is not designed to replace or take the place of any form of medicine or professional medical advice. The information in this ebook has been provided for educational & entertainment purposes only.

The information contained in this book has been compiled from sources deemed reliable, and it is accurate to the best of the Author's knowledge; however, the Author cannot guarantee its accuracy and validity and cannot be held liable for any errors or omissions. Changes are periodically made to this book. You must consult your doctor or get professional medical advice before using any of the suggested remedies, techniques, or information in this book.

TABLE OF CONTENTS

Introduction

I would like to acknowledge and congratulate you for obtaining this book. The fact that your choice to purchase this guide is a sign that you're determined to increase your earnings potential. This guide is designed to help you achieve this.

Work as a freelancer is becoming the norm. Many are choosing jobs that can be done at home. The possibilities are endless, but they can be overwhelming. You might be just beginning or already have experience working online. Perhaps you require a major source of income or require an additional job to make cash, and obtaining online jobs is a smart choice.

As with many other workers, you've likely dreamed of working at your home. You are dreading the commute because due to the anxiety and amount of time you spend getting to and from work. In addition working out everywhere demands you to manage numerous personalities and lots of drama at work. Who hasn't been astonished by the gossip of their colleagues about each other or shared their

1

frustrations about the way they're treated in their lives? It's enough to want to be away from all of it.

In the current time, it's not a dream anymore. Finding jobs online is an issue of survival for the majority of people. Many were laid off from their jobs, while some find it difficult to find work due to restrictions on their movement.

In the present market, you can discover a wide range of tasks which can be completed easily by using the Internet and computers.

It is crucial to remember that being freelancers isn't more straightforward than working from home. When it comes to actual work it is essential to dedicate yourself completely to your accomplishment. While you may think it's easier to remain focused after you've rid yourself of those annoying coworkers as well as your boss, there will be numerous problems you'll need to overcome when working online for yourself.

Find out what that will help you get started as a freelancer who is just starting out.

Chapter 1: Freelance Vs. Remote Job Position

For this section, we'll discuss freelance and remote work. We will attempt to distinguish between these two terms and also discuss what are the advantages as well as cons of working at home.

Remote work is an employment arrangement where employees do not have to commute or go to their central place of work, like an office building or warehouse. Telework is also referred to as teleworking, telework and telecommuting, it is a mobile work, and a flexible workplaces. Employers can be able to take on a full-time job at a firm and work from home. They are considered full-time employees for the company and may work outside of the traditional office setting. If you are interested in remote jobs applicants must provide a resume or CV and the cover letter. Candidates will then be approached by the company hiring to schedule an interview.

As opposed to remote jobs that are freelance, work for freelancers is dependent. The contract you sign with the client or company ends when the project is complete. In the majority of cases these are part-time positions where the freelancers are able to complete the majority or even all of the project. The freelancer is self-employed and not an employee of a firm. When applying for a position as a freelancer the freelancer must make proposals or bids that explain their reasons for being selected for the job. The freelancer will usually be paid either per hour or per day to perform their duties.

Once you have figured out the primary distinction between the two ideas, it's simple to decide the kind of thing you're seeking.

Benefits of working as a freelancer

Freedom to choose which the clients or projects you want to be working on

One of the greatest advantages of being freelancer is freedom to choose. It allows you to pick what type of project you would like to tackle. It is easy to choose which job interests you the most.

Excellent location Flexibility

When you are a freelancer, it is possible to are able to work from anywhere anytime. You don't have to fret about getting to work or resuming work in a physical site. If you've got an internet connection and an iPhone or personal computer you will earn money while you work.

Faster growth benefits

You can collaborate with employers all over the world which helps in developing inter-personal and network skills. When you work as a freelancer you have the opportunity to develop your skills and abilities. You are not restricted by a specific workplace structure or arrangement. An employee who is freelance can be hired by the business as a full-time worker remote jobs.

Remote and freelancing jobs are increasing and more businesses say they prefer hiring freelancers or remote worker, as it assists in reducing overhead costs in office spaces.

The biggest challenge to working online

It could require longer duration of time

Employees who work online have to approach their jobs the same way as any other job. Making sure you are able to commit to the job, if not physically, but mentally is essential. Online jobs aren't an opportunity to sit back and relax at your home. In reality, you might have to put in more effort, usually working longer hours than in a traditional job, to earn similar amounts of cash, particularly at the beginning. Once you've established your online career , you'll enjoy the advantages of being able work from home, or any other location you prefer. But, getting there requires patience and time.

At the beginning you must first identify the appropriate kind of job and the ideal employer. As with many job seekers who are online You've probably been a victim of shady online jobs. People who pay hundreds of dollars to start online jobs only to not be paid for their work are all over the Internet. There are numerous stories of scams in which employees work for a company that appears to be their own and never get any money for their work. Avoid these unpleasant circumstances by selecting your job and employers carefully.

Are highly competitive

Many people are seeking work online. Due to the current conditions that are happening, there are more online employees as than there ever was. As jobs are being posted every day, more workers are willing to take on the job. If you are planning to work from home, you have to be able to stand out from people who are similar to you. You need to be able attract the attention of clients and provide them with outcomes that keep them coming back. That means you have to be able to demonstrate an income-generating skill and offer clients high-quality jobs that keep them coming back.

The uncertain

A freelancer's work is often fraught with uncertainties. They must rely on themselves when finding an appropriate client. Their source of earnings isn't reliable as competitiveness is very high. The majority of workers prefer remote work because they are more secure than freelance work.

It's not an easy task especially if you're just beginning your journey. You must be prepared to work hard. Beware of false ads that claim to give you an easy solution. PUT IN THE WORK TO GET RESULTS.

Chapter Summary.

Then, in this section we discussed the distinctions between remote work as well as freelance work. We also talked about the benefits and disadvantages of working at home.

In the next section, we'll go over the steps to follow when selecting an online job. We will look at the factors to look for and ways to tell whether a legitimate client is fraud.

Chapter 2: Tips To Choose Online Employment

In the final section, we looked at remote jobs and freelance work. We talked about their differences as well as the advantages of working online.

The next chapter we'll discuss the aspects to be aware of when applying for an online job. We will discuss the most the most popular scams and ways to locate a genuine job which will pay.

There are numerous channels through which you can find remote or freelance work. Since the market is extremely competitive, it is essential to to work hard to find a customer. Before you begin making your first move, pay careful attention to these suggestions. They can keep you from spending time and money looking for the incorrect sources.

There is no need to make a payment to have an idea

Do not pay for the first time you work with an employer online. The legitimate online businesses doesn't need you to contribute your own cash to begin. There might be expenses for you, such as upgrading your computer equipment or software however, they are purely a matter of preference and not an obligation to work online.

An experience I have had personally was by a customer who approached me about writing work. The contact was made through a reputable freelance website and the terms offered looked very promising. The client provided me with an outline of the articles they wanted for me to work on. The compensation was excellent and the site appeared legitimate and I was willing to do my best until the client requested I pay him a tiny amount prior to being given the task. According to this client the fee was a "security cost which will be refunded to me following the conclusion of the task. The fee was intended to guarantee that I'd deliver and protect his work.

If you come into contact with clients who behave this way run away. There is nothing more alarming more than a client who asks you to make a payment to get an assignment. Don't fall for this.

Beware of frauds

Don't fall for frauds. You're a smart individual. Keep in mind that if something seems too amazing to be true, you're probably right. If you are looking to earn money online, you'll need to do the work.

"Get rich" programs are often empty claims made to take advantage of people's greed and misconceptions that there are quick ways to wealth. If you're not planning to win the lottery and bet on becoming rich quickly. There aren't any secrets to making money tomorrow or even earning a million dollars within about three months. Also, you can't make money doing nothing. If you truly desire to earn money online, do your best to earn it.

Do background checks

Review references and checks for background. Anyone can claim they're a legitimate business but they need to be legitimate to be able to prove that. Investigate any company that offers work. Review their references and look in to their background. If you are thinking of being employed by a certain individual or company do not just visit the site. Search for them on Google and learn the most you can about them prior to accepting even one job.

If you work for an individual and they don't pay you or aren't able to pay you on time, you should not do business with them in the future.

There are many great online employers who pay you in time. Doing nothing but focusing on fraudsters on the Internet can only bring your mental strength down.

I was once duped by a customer because I did not study my material prior to starting the task. The client in question asked me to write eight affiliate articles that were three thousand words per. To make sure he was paid, I asked the client to establish milestone payments prior to me starting (milestone/escrow the payment process is used as a safety measure used by freelance websites where clients pay a set amount which will be paid out to the freelancer after the project is finished. Both freelancers and clients typically will agree to any number of milestones they'd like prior to work beginning. In this way, you're both secure)

But, the client saw that I had not been on the site and made use of my ignorance. He sent me an extensive message that stated he had already given me the project and , therefore I didn't have anything to worry about. Since I was in desperate need of an opportunity and was in desperate need of cash so I threw caution to the wind and began the work. I had already submitted 4 articles in total and was set to submit the fifth when I realized that the account of my client was deleted. I called customer service and was told the account was deleted after they realized the freelancer was scamming other freelancers through the website.

A sad story. I put a lot of effort into the project as I wanted to give my best, but I was scammed. It was a difficult time during my freelance career and I wouldn't want anyone else to repeat the same error. Again, if something appears too appealing and seems too good to be so, make sure you check and then check over and over again.

Be sure to read the conditions and terms of any freelancer you sign up with and also the security measures that are generally, there is a milestone payment. There are many websites are legitimate but they're also vulnerable to fraudsters looking for ignorant freelancers to profit from. Beware.

You must ensure that you provide high-quality outcomes

If you're just beginning your journey one way to make yourself stand out is to do your all. Be the best that you can each day. Work hard and you will reap the rewards, in any profession. The more hard you work the more you will be visible plus the harder work you'll need to perform. It may seem that some jobs aren't as important as others, but you don't have a clue where this may take you. Although the internet may seem like a huge space there is a good chance that you'll meet mutual acquaintances. If you've got a great reputation, it will be followed by others. A good reputation can lead to better pay and favorable reviews.

It isn't important how big or small the undertaking may appear. Make sure to meet your promises and deliver. Customers will leave glowing reviews of a freelancer who is willing to go the extra mile, which will keep them coming back. Don't accept any task that you don't have the ability to complete. Be sure to ask questions before you send out bids or proposals to get clarification. Customers love freelancers who are open and genuinely committed to their work, so do not be afraid to ask questions.

These steps can serve as a guideline when you are searching for the ideal online job. Although you've heard numerous negative stories, getting an online job that is legitimate isn't as difficult as appears with the right mindset and the right knowledge. The trick is finding an appropriate job that is filled with appropriate people. It doesn't matter if you be employed by someone else, or go into the business on your own, you'll need to be skilled in distinguishing those who are reliable from those that do not.

Chapter Summary.

Then, in this section we discussed how to search for high-quality online jobs as well as how to identify fraudulent websites.

In the next installment, we'll discuss the most popular online jobs as well as the prerequisites for getting started with any of them.

Chapter 3: Popular Online Jobs

In the previous chapter, we covered how to get jobs on the internet.

In this section we will talk about the most sought-after jobs on the internet and what's required to be able to fulfill any one of them.

Customer Service Jobs

Customer service jobs are one of the very few jobs available online that require no special abilities. All you require is a computer that works as well as the Internet connection.

As a representative for service You can be employed by one of the many companies that provide customer support via online contractors. The services you could offer depending on your experience could include: answering simple questions or registering customers, making orders, or giving technical advice regarding products.

Many businesses employ online and at-home employees. You can work for an airline or an Internet service, a catalog business, an entrepreneur who is successful and many more. The possibilities are endless.

Find a Legitimate Customer Service job

The most reliable place to search for an excellent job is the job marketplace online. Websites such as Upwork, Fiverr and Guru have strict rules for their members. The number of jobs posted on these sites is astounding and, with a little some digging through, sorting and weeding I can't see a reason to not get work quickly.

Be sure to always utilize the online Escrow payment service to make sure you get paid. Escrow is a secure intermediary between you and your employer.

After they have chosen the job advertised for you Your new employer will make the amount agreed upon into Escrow. Then, you will be informed via email. When you are aware that the funds have been allocated, you are now able to start your job. Don't begin work until you've been informed about this. Believe me when I say that I've been there and have made hundreds of dollars loss in the process when the client vanished with my excellent work and did not pay me.

Starting as an Service Rep

To get started with this type of job you'll need an offer or resume you can make available online. Like you'd expect, obtaining an online job is usually an issue of sending a lot of emails and making phone calls to potential employers.

It is very likely that you'll never have the opportunity to meet your boss or coworkers face-to-face. Be sure your resume shows your interpersonal abilities as well as any related customer service jobs you've had previously. Should this be a major career shift for you, it could be beneficial to find an employment as a customer service representative in a retail establishment to improve your abilities. Because this could be a challenge in the present it is also possible to earn knowledge by volunteering to work for family members and friends who run online businesses for no cost.

Of course, you'll be required to ensure your resume is correct in grammar because you may be required to submit your reports online or via email. Computer skills are an absolute requirement.

A majority of businesses will require that applicants have a basic understanding of the programs they use most often. They typically use spreadsheet and word processing applications. Keep in mind that your job will not only be handling customers, but it also requires you to write reports regarding your tasks. Therefore, you must be familiar with the most common software programs for computers.

If you're not proficient with these programs, you can learn online or enroll in specific classes to make sure that you're prepared to deal with everything that may come your way. Visit sites such as Coursera, Edx, Udemy and more for online courses that will improve your abilities.

Stay with what you know/like

While browsing through the numerous websites that advertise online jobs in customer service, you should focus only on the jobs that appeal to you. If you are offered a job where you'll be spending a lot of hours every day speaking with people about the service or product your company offers. As such, it is important to ensure that you're interested in the subject you will be discussing.

For example, if you are a travel enthusiast, you could be interested in working as a travel agent or an airline travel agency. Your understanding of travel as well as the thrill you could offer clients is an important benefit to you.

If you're skilled in the field, you could be a great candidate to work for the Internet service provider or any other technology firm. If you select jobs that match your skills and expertise employers will spend less time to train you. You will also be pushed up the list of candidates.

If you enjoy being with people and aiding them, then every job in customer service is a good fit for you. In actual fact, to succeed in this area of work you must have excellent interpersonal skills, a desire to spend time to each client (so they feel taken care of) and a genuine passion for the business with which you work. While not all customer service jobs involve direct contact with the public Some work from a business business viewpoint.

Perform a preferred search

If you're interested in a certain for a specific keyword, lookup to find "inside customer services" (business to business) and "outside customer support" that refers to dealing on behalf of the public.

Profit from the Second Language Skills

One of the biggest advantages of the job of a customer service representative is that you can speak a different language. There are a lot of bilingual customer service positions in waiting for applicants to apply. Be aware that these positions require an absolute proficiency in the language of the area of concern. This is why they are paid a handsome sum too.

The main thing you need to do to get a customer service position is to be passionate in your business or your products. If you are able to do that, your clients will be satisfied and so will your boss.

Issue of burning out

One of the possible issues that can arise from working in this type of work is the burnout syndrome. If you have to deal with an abundance of clients every day (and often angry customers) it's not difficult to become exhausted after a certain amount of time.

If you feel that your work isn't satisfying, don't quit. Learn more about the business and the products it offers. This will be helpful when you try to assist customers on the phone. If you are still wanting to quit consider other jobs in customer service which will better fit your style of work. If you're working out-of-the-box customer services, change onto inside services, and reverse the process. It is not necessary to remain with the first position you are offered. Being around people can be stressful, but it's also highly satisfying. If you find yourself in an issue even with the best intentions, it's best to quit before you harm the reputation of your company and waste your time.

Data Entry Jobs

If you'd rather not handle customers such as a data entry position, it could be the ideal career for you. Unfortunately, it's an occupation that has been the subject of a variety of scams getting into the market.

Due to the sheer number of scams being perpetrated in the field it's becoming extremely difficult for you or anyone else, to locate an authentic online job for data entry. There are legitimate companies searching for experts in data entry.

Businesses save lots of money when they employ people who work at home. They do not have to cover the expenses of residing an entire team of clerks for data entry and also don't have to invest money in maintaining many computer equipment. This means that you, the home-based professional who handles data entry, the perfect candidate for this.

Good Pay Rates

Do not fret; you will not have to pay for these costs by working at your home. While you'll need to cover your own equipment for computers as well as you will also have to pay for your Internet connection, and any other equipment related to office that you decide to make use of, you don't need to shell out an enormous amount of money to be able to working at home.

Data entry jobs can are very lucrative because businesses are able to reduce costs by not paying massive overhead costs. Most of these employers have those who are like you. They could even be a single-person operation for themselves.

Additionally to that, when you have a data entry job , you'll be able the opportunity to work from home. This lets you enjoy the freedom that you've always wanted and even working while wearing only your underwear.

Are you suited to this line of Work?

It is important to be aware of the work load and time required to earn money from data entry. If you're not capable processing data fast, you may not be suitable for this kind of work. It's also helpful to you to be focused and stay away from interruptions from the outside to finish the job.

Entry of information can become a chore. It could be a tedious task to fill out reports, writing letters, or filling in endless databases, documents, or lists. It is possible to transcribe minutes or books from meetings. The information you receive is likely to be of little or nothing to you, which is beneficial. If you're the kind of person who is unable to pack bags, or tidy your home without becoming distracted the field of data entry may not be your ideal field. In order to do the job correctly, you must be totally detached from the actual information. You must be motivated by getting the data in as quick as you can without pride or prejudice towards its content. Additionally, you should be able to complete the task error-free.

The online job of data entry is ideal for anyone who is not looking to interact with lots of others since you'll work on your own. The ideal candidate happens to be a skilled typing expert who can block out the world to finish their job. If you're among the people listed above who are competent to conduct the study to locate the perfect online data entry job.

Online Transcription Jobs

Similar to transcription is a job that requires data entry. The major difference between transcription and data entry is the degree of expertise required. Transcription jobs require more experience and a bit of training to be able to do them efficiently. Schools of trade and vocational training typically provide courses in legal, medical as well as financial, transcription.

Take a look at certification

If you're interested in doing transcription online, you ought to consider becoming certified. You'll need to pay some money for these courses however in the end, it will be worth the cost.

If you are looking for jobs on the internet Look for companies who require certification or have expertise in transcription. These companies tend to be more genuine that means you're more likely to be paid. They might also request you to complete an online test of transcription and rate your precision and speed. Professional transcription companies require people who are able to complete the task in a short time. It is highly recommended to learn to type prior to applying for a job in transcription.

What's the deal?

The work of a transcriptionist involves listening to recordings of meetings and notes and then making reports from them. You might be provided with recordings of notes taken by patients from doctors, notes from legal documents recorded by attorneys, and notes taken by accountants.

All this information has to be entered into a report, so that it is able to be saved in the patient or client file. Every report needs to be written in a particular format. Employers have their own requirements regarding these formats, so it is important to be aware of these formats as soon as you can to avoid delays that are unnecessary.

Exemple Process

If you're writing the report of a doctor there is a chance that you'll be able to hear the numbers of the vital signs of the patient. The next item to be discussed is the purpose of the visit and the subsequent conversation between the physician and patient.

There are also notes about the course of treatment and details about the prescriptions for the patient. This information is needed so that doctors and nurses are able to quickly and easily go through the patient's records to learn about their medical history, regardless of whether it's their first time. A good chart is also helpful in the event that the office must invoice insurers or Medicare. If you work in this field, you must be knowledgeable about the intricacies of medical terminology and spelling, so that your reports are precise and reliable.

You might be required to use specific equipment when you perform transcriptions. The recordings will need to be played through your PC, which means you'll need to purchase specific software. Additionally, you'll require a comfortable, high-quality headset to listen to recordings. The headset you wear for a long time so purchasing a more expensive headset is well worth the price.

Freelance Writing

Writing for free is among the most accessible online careers. If you are familiar with the basics on the Internet you will know how websites get ranked based on their content. If you conduct a search using keywords, those words are linked with websites that have keywords that match the keywords you typed in.

To ensure that their sites get the top search engine rankings webmasters are working hard to make sure their sites are stocked with relevant and fresh information. As you can imagine the task of writing all that content is typically outsourced by freelancers.

There are a variety of categories that fall under freelance writing. It is recommended to choose a specific area of interest and focus on it. Customers are more likely to work with freelancers who excel at their job, therefore don't try to appear to be all-encompassing.

Low Start-Up Costs

If you love to write and you have a few writing skills, then this position could be ideal for you. The only prerequisites needed for a writing freelance job is a computer as well as an understanding of English. English language.

Freedom of writing freelance

There are many online job websites offer freelance writing services for eager service providers. Try online job sites like Upwork, Fiverr or freelancer.com Find posts on a forum or on specific sites.

It is possible to offer work for you to work on a piece-by- per piece or on a per-project basis. Based on the work that you are working on, you may work with ten employers per day (writing an article every day) or get an article writing job for one company, earning enough to allow you to work fullor part time.

Keep Yourself Organized

No matter how many employers you work for regardless of how many employers you have, it is essential to come up with ways to keep track of every aspect of your work and earnings. Due to how freelance writers work, having organizing skills can help you save time and make sure you get paid. One advantage of making use of a trusted website for finding work is that you are able to talk to other writers about employers. They'll be able to determine if you pay punctually or if their pay is not as fast.

Any website with importance will have strict guidelines about payment. Certain websites allow users to pay in private, usually via PayPal and others take care of your payment using Escrow services. Whatever you choose so long as you've tracked your earnings and work thoroughly , you should have recourse options in the event that you are not paid or you are paid less than the amount that was agreed upon.

Monetize Experience

If you're an expert in a certain subject, you may also write and publish articles yourself. There are numerous sites for article marketing which accept submissions, and make them available for others to read. These articles may be linked to a specific website, and create an income stream for you. Additionally, they can assist to establish your brand. It is crucial to promote your brand and provide an impressive portfolio that you can refer to when searching for work. Although it may not be a huge amount of money at first but it will eventually bring an excellent and consistent stream of income.

Learn to become a Pro-Blogger

Articles aren't the only method to earn money through freelance writing. You can also create blog posts that are slightly easier to write and pay as well. Pro-blogging is paying for blogging services. Since the advent of the Internet blogs have popped up on the market in the same way as a mushrooms in a rain-soaked forest.

Blog posts are typically written with more authority yet they remain engaging and entertaining. If you've visited the fan sites, you may be aware that they have blogs. A majority of instances, these blogs aren't written by the webmaster who is actually writing them or even by the person they have hired.

How to Prepare Yourself For the job at hand

If you're thinking about writing for a freelance basis as a career , you'll need have writing samples on hand. Make sure that no one who is determined to hire you will hire you immediately without reviewing your work.

Every freelance site requires that you have a solid portfolio that outlines the tasks you've worked on previously.

You are free to write a few article or blog posts, as examples.

It is a given that you should be able to write well in order for potential employer, however you must understand how online-based writing functions. Many writers on the internet aren't native English native English speakers. This may be detrimental to them in the long run, but the old saying about the inability to identify as an English native speaker has less weight. What is important is the result of the work.

You need to be proficient in writing clearly and concisely style. Your writing should be simple to read and understand. To gain a better understanding of the market you want for, it is suggested to spend time on the internet. There are some good and bad examples as you the research. This can help you decide the most effective alternative when it comes down to the work you will be delivering.

Look up popular blogs to gain an understanding of their style of writing and then model the style of your own style. Be aware that customers will not like your work if they feel it's not unique. Your content must be unique, error-free and Google search engine optimized. This means that you should include keywords relevant to aid your website's ranking highly. Find out more about SEO writing or enroll in an online course through Udemy, Edx or Coursera to gain an understanding.

Start small.

As you begin your journey, you'll probably need to take on any job that comes your way, usually with a low salary. Once you've made yourself known, you will be able to receive a extra pay for your work and start to accumulate an ongoing stream of work. To reach this stage, you'll have work hard and be a great writer. writing. Be sure that everything you write is of the highest quality, even for smaller assignments that pay less. Remember that your reputation at stake if you do not provide quality content.

The field that freelance writers can work in is open and is achievable without any initial costs. You will be working many hours in order to start your company. It is also essential to love writing, no matter what topic you choose, since you'll do a lot of writing.

Personal skills aren't as crucial to be successful in this position however they are helpful. It is still necessary to be able to communicate with people.

Virtual Assistant

The role as a virtual assistant an extremely awaited and lucrative online jobs. Virtual assistants are an entrepreneur, who performs contracts for other businesses. Most likely, you'll be self-employed, meaning you'll also need to advertise your services to other companies. This isn't easy and is best suited for those who have experience as administrative professionals. In the beginning , you'll likely have to put in long hours to get your venture on the right track. It's not easy to begin but the reward could be enormous.

Sell Your Skills

One of the most important things to think about if you're seeking to become an assistant virtual is the specific collection of abilities. Did you have previous experience in human resources or in marketing? Did you work as a travel agent or a real estate agent? Have you worked in bookkeeping or finance?

The more specific you are with your offerings, the better likelihood that you'll identify a niche you want to pursue, and businesses that require your expertise. For instance, if you have worked as an accountant for a couple of years, you can advertise yourself as an online bookkeeper. This opens the door to customers who have small businesses that need bookkeeping services.

In the same way, if you were a travel agent, you could be able to offer assistance with travel for large corporations. In both cases, the business will benefit as all they need to pay you. They don't have to offer a benefits package or office space for you. This will save the company money. A majority of your work can be completed on the Internet.

It is crucial to conduct some research prior to starting out. It is important to know expectations are expected of you by your employer with regard to working hours and money made. It is likely that your clients may not be located in the same time zone, and you could need to work late into the midnight or even very late in the day. The upside is that this may also open up time during your time for your. The virtual assistant job is perfect for parents who have small children wanting to spend more moments with toddlers.

What you need to bring to the Table to be an Assistant Virtual

In contrast to other positions listed This one is more demanding to be proficient in writing and interpersonal communication abilities. If you aren't able to demonstrate the two skills, or aren't comfortable with people you don't know regularly, then this job not the right fit for you.

Tech jobs in the field of technology

The first step towards becoming fully your boss is to obtain an array of highly sought-after abilities. Skills in technology are among the skills that are sought-after that employers are looking for across the world.

Companies are always on search for app and website designers to assist in the design of their projects.

You can also find a wide range of opportunities for designers on the internet. This includes web design, graphics design animators, voiceovers, and other things. The list of possibilities is endless. The majority of these jobs are well-paying and can be accomplished in a the shortest time.

If you don't have any expertise, it could be the perfect time to acquire one. The best way to begin is by looking up the most the most popular jobs on the internet by using the websites listed. Pay attention to the competencies they offer and pick one or more skills to study. The next step is to go to sites such as Udemy, Coursera, etc and master a new ability. It is possible to learn an entire new skill in two months or less if you're committed.

Chapter 4: How To Find Online Job Positions

In the previous chapter, we covered the most popular jobs on the internet and the various requirements they require.

This chapter we'll discuss ways to locate online work and develop the latest skills.

How do you find jobs online

* Go online to search for work-related job open positions (see the list below)

* Use the search feature on LinkedIn for jobs on the internet (remote or freelance) jobs.

• Ensure that you've put together an effective portfolio, resume, and cover letters

Your portfolio contains examples of work you've done over the years. If you're just starting out, make your own samples and then post them on portfolio websites such as Behance (website designer) or use clippings. In this way, you can include the link to your portfolio every time you're making proposals or sending cover letters.

Your cover letter must explain the reasons you are interested in the job and demonstrate your strengths and the value you're planning to add to the organization.

* Learn the relevant qualifications and skills.

Create a compelling profile Your profile gives you the chance to impress on potential clients. One good way to do this is to research the top freelancers in your area and use their profiles to create a model for your own.

• Send out robust proposals Your proposal should be an introduction letter. It must demonstrate your expertise and what you're willing to provide to customers. You must tailor every proposition you submit to meet the specific requirements of your job. Do not just duplicate the same proposal to multiple clients. Include the essential skills that the client requires for in their job description. Let them know why you're the best option for them.

* Avoid using generic abilities as it discourages customers. Pick a niche you are specialized in and do your best in it. For instance, if you're a writer pick a subject which is specific e.g. commercial writing the writing of resumes, SEO and so on. Clients prefer hiring specialists rather than generic freelancers.

Finding a job online is heavily dependent on the qualifications you can provide. Employers are more interested in the skills you have than in your educational background. That's why it's crucial to concentrate on a particular skill, master it and be ready to provide top-quality work to your customers.

Here are some websites that can help you acquire new techniques:

Coursera

Khan academy

EdX

Udemy

MIT opencourseware

Codecademy

Open culture online courses

TED-Ed

You can also use Google to search for additional websites by typing in keywords that are relevant of the specific skills you would like to master.

Here are the most sought-after capabilities on the most popular freelance platforms:

Android developer Data scientist PHP developer

Facebook developer Mobile app developer Graphic designer

Content writer Analyst of Information Security Java developer

Bookkeeper Ios developer Enterprise architecture

Copywriter Product photography Google app engine

Customer service representative Google cloud Platform Resume Writer

Customer retention Block chain Sales consultant

Game developer Virtual assistant Go developer

Web designer Technical writer Apple UIkit

Microsoft Wordpress Developer Software Engineer Apple Xcode

SEO Writer Social media manager Block chain

UI/UX designer eLearning Tensor flow

Volusion Drop Box API Genetic algorithms

iPhone UI design Vue js. ScoRM

Proposal writing Oculus rift Vuforia

HR consulting Microsoft power BI Instructional design

Here are the platforms that offer remote or freelance services:

http://flexjobs.com

https://weworkremotely.com

https://remote.co/remote-jobs/

http://remotive.io

http://skipthedrive.com

http://virtualvocations.com

https://remoteok.io

http://workingnomads.co

https://jobspresso.co

http://europeremotely.com

http://jobscribe.com

https://wfh.io

https://outsourcely.com/remoteworker

http://powertofly.com

https://landing.jobs/

http://authenticjobs.com

https://t.co/5BWU2jxnXl?amp=

http://careers.stackoverflow.com

https://t.co/8r5Jx7bQPT?amp=

https://toptal.com/business

https://fiverr.com

https://upwork.com

http://guru.com

https://freelancer.com

http://freelancermap.com

https://coworks.com

https://gun.io/#hacker

https://themuse.com/jobs

http://indeed.com

http://careerbuilder.com

http://idealist.org

https://members.solidgigs.com/

https://talent.hubstaff.com/

https://remotees.com/

https://100telecommutejobs.com/telejobs/

https://workew.com/

https://www.cloudpeeps.com/

https://remote4me.com/

https://werk.co/

You can also look on twitter or LinkedIn for job openings on freelance.

Landing A Good Remote Job

1. Apply only for positions you are qualified for: It is essential to be aware of all the requirements prior to applying for any job. If you're looking to acquire an extremely sought-after ability, you can use any of the listed resources to study.

2. Follow all directions given Since companies receive a lot of applications for each job ad An easy method to identify candidates is to check those who did not follow the directions that are provided. Be aware of any specific specifications and modify accordingly.

3. Make sure you submit a professional resume. It's essential to submit an impressive resume that will draw the attention of the prospective employer. Most recruiters will spend less than 10

seconds perusing your resume. Therefore, yours needs to be captivating. Be sure to remove unnecessary information and customize your resume to suit every job you're applying for.

4. Create a compelling cover letter or personal statement Your cover letter needs to convince the employer that you're the perfect candidate to the position. In this section, you should discuss the skills you're hoping to contribute to the organization and the reason reasons why you're drawn to that particular company.

Freelance Work

There are many platforms that allow freelance work that has been previously described. Some of the most popular include Upwork, Fiverr, freelancer.com and many more. To be a freelancer on one of them, you need to establish a solid profile that will attract the attention of potential clients.

PROFILE

Freelancers must submit bids or proposals when applying to a project. If a prospective client views their proposal, then the first step they do is check your profile. Your profile needs to convince them that you're a suitable candidate for their project, and encourage them to open the conversation.

An effective method to create an impressive profile is to look at top-earning people in your industry and copy your profile from their profile. Look up about 10 freelancers for a decent idea of the ideal profile to be like.

SECTIONS ELECTRIC

1. Professional photo: When creating your profile, make sure that you use a professional image. It should be a smiley headshot of yourself in an outfit for business with a simple background. Do not use selfies or large pictures.

2. Titles and taglines These are the places where you describe your personal experience and preferences in a concise and concise format.

3. Overview It is the place the place where you describe what you are doing, your past experiences, and the relevant abilities.

4. Work experience and education In the event that you've got any relevant experience related to your field, make sure to list them here.

5. Portfolio The portfolio is a crucial section because it's the thing that convinces clients of your expertise. Your portfolio should include examples of work you've done before. If you're a novice you should create a few samples of your work for utilize.

Your portfolio gives you the opportunity to share your story and create your reputation. It is essential to focus on the most important items that are related to your specialization. However ensure that the audience to get a glimpse of who you are.

Be sure to shut down your profile and ask clients to take you on immediately.

PROPOSALS

Freelancers must submit bids or proposals when seeking work. The cover letter is sent to the client. It must be enticing.

Before you write a proposal, review the details of the project and consider the needs of the customer. It is then possible to think about how you are going to meet these requirements within your proposals. The proposal you submit should not be long and concentrate on the requirements of the client and how you intend to apply your knowledge to solving these issues.

It could also be necessary to include relevant examples or hyperlinks to your proposal. Do not send out generic proposals. Customize each proposal to suit the position to the position to which you're applying.

RESUMES, COVERLETTERS AND PROPOSALS

When you apply for remote jobs You will need to provide your resume and cover letter. Since employers receive a lot of applications for each job opening You must make sure that your cover letter and resume stand out.

It is not necessary to spend thousands of dollars to create a great CV or cover letter. There are plenty of online for free CV template and letter of cover examples. There are sites that aid in the review of your resume or CV.

Here are some examples of resumes and CV builders:

Zety

Novoresume

ResumeOK

VisualCV

SlashCV

Resumption

CVmaker

Kick off

Resume builder

Resume Genius

Myperfectresume

Enhancv

Resume review sites

Rezscore

Vmock

Skillroads

COVER LIST SAMPLES

Sample 1

Hello,

I am writing to respond to your job posting for the job of a Writer.

Over the last three years, I have worked as a freelancer for various brands and organizations across different sectors, I believe that my skills along with my professional education are a great fit for this job. In my previous roles I've had:

Created hundreds of blog articles and posts for companies across a variety of industries.

Searched for keywords and adhered to strict SEO guidelines.

Content that has been created that is 100 100% unique and completely error-free.

Utilized key software to measure the practices of industry and adapting content to meet.

Beyond my technical abilities beyond my technical skills, I'm an excellent communicator, and an experienced leader with abilities to traverse through the digital landscape and adapt to its ever-changing requirements.

Attached to the note is my résumé, which describes my professional background and experiences, as well as how they pertain to the position. I am confident and confident that I will become a valuable member of your team.

Sample 2

RE Web Content Developer

Dear Sir/Ma

As I was searching for new opportunities in the field of creativity I was thrilled to see the Web Content Developer opening at Chevko LLC. As a highly motivated professional with expertise in proofreading and writing I think I'd be a fantastic member of your team.

Finding better ways to approach and improved solutions to business problems are the things that motivate and motivate me. I am extremely driven and proud of my ability to come up with new ways of thinking. I believe that fresh ideas and experimenting with new methods will help companies grow.

Contributions to my previous Freelance Content Writer role, and the entire field focus on my core skills in managing deadlines and writing. I have developed excellent communication skills and have gained an extensive experience as a major contributor due to my analytical thinking and problem-solving abilities.

I've written hundreds of blog posts for a broad spectrum of industries. I also wrote website copy as well as social media content, and other promotional materials that span a wide fields of specialization. They include dating, lifestyle interior design relationships, science business, technology and finance. Not only has my knowledge helped me develop my abilities, but I've also gained knowledge about SEO practices that can assist my clients to achieve their goals for marketing.

To get a better understanding of my professional background and experience Please take a look at my resume. I've also included writing samples of work I have done previously. I would love to talk with you about this possibility and am grateful for your interest.

Sincerely,

Samuel Joseph.

Sample 3

Dear Ms. Potter,

I would like to apply for the job of Web Designer advertised via dayjob.com. dayjob.com website.

I will utilize the technical as well as non-technical abilities to create high-quality websites that are distinctive from the rest.

According to your specifications, I am up-to-date with the most current internet trends, techniques and technology. I am also an expert in cross-browser compatibility finding out technical requirements as well as creating backup files, resolving code issues and creating digital interfaces that are interactive.

My current job requires me to am part of a tight and integrated team of software delivery. My duties include web design, logos and interfaces and development of online marketing, emails and social media channel content. Furthermore, I am involved in developing the business's policies and procedures on concerns of confidentiality as well as Data Protection.

The CV attached will showcase my breadth, my quality and my love for design. These factors make me an ideal candidate to the position you are seeking.

Personally, I am fully aware of the pressures and deadlines that come with the studio environment and believe I've got the stamina and determination to produce results in this kind of environment.

In the present I am in search of the right job that will allow me to be an integral element of a fast-growing company. I would love the chance to discuss my experience and talents in greater depth with you. I am willing to meet with you whenever you are available. To conclude, I'd appreciate your reviewing my application.

Thank you very much,

August Alsina

Sample 4

Thank you, Madame. Henson,

I am writing to submit my application for the virtual assistant position with Compact LLC. I have seven years of work experience working as a virtual assistant. I love the variety of work it offers every day.

As a virtual assistant freelance I provide a variety of services to my clients like document preparation, keeping records and files. My experience with a range of computer programs allows me to effortlessly complete any task assigned to me. I'm a fast learner and enjoy challenges too. As a meticulous and organized professional , I am proud of completing my assignments in a timely manner and with precision. I can type up to 100 words per minute, and possess exceptional communication skills, both in writing and verbal. I would like the chance to bring these abilities into Synergy Systems as your Virtual Assistant.

I'm self-motivated and have an entire home office setup. Therefore, I'm eager to start working for you as your personal assistant quickly as I can. I'd like to invite you to get in touch with me to schedule an interview at the earliest time. Thank you for your consideration and time.

Sincerely,

Abigail Joseph

PROPOSAL SAMPLES for freelance work

1)

Hi,

I can see that you're searching for a well-established blog writer , and I would be happy to lend you my writing expertise.

As a writer and a creative mind, I'd be thrilled to make use of my talents to connect with your audience! I'm able to write about many different topics and can modify my style of writing to suit.

My blog posts are thoroughly researched, unique and SEO-friendly. As an author, I know the need for original content that shatters the Google algorithms and grabs the your readers' interest simultaneously.

It's easily to talk to and I'm driven to provide engaging content. Here's a link to my portfolio.

I truly believe that my work will be able to speak for itself and that this will be the beginning of a long-term business relationship. We hope that I will hear from you shortly!

Thank you for your consideration,

Samuel.

2)

Dear Employer,

You've indicated that you require an experienced proofreader to review and revise your writing (blogs Press Releases, guest articles). I provide grammatically correct and consistent results for proofreading requirements and ensure you that the tone and voice remain consistent.

A service you can count to for quick service and high-quality. I am an experienced native English speaker who holds an associate's degree. Because of my focus on detail and a meticulous approach I will ensure that the work you do is done efficiently and precisely.

Best Regards,

David.

3)

Hi Leo,

I am able to write blog articles on your Amazon niche websites. I've written a number of posts on health, home beauty, gardening, and other related niches. I'll share with you during the chat.

How many documents will you require? What is the deadline for your submission? Please share it with me on the chat.

Your content will be of excellent quality, exceptional great English thoroughly researched 100% original, unique, and will be able to pass Copyscape. I will adhere to your instructions and submit your work by the timeframe.

I am an Native English Content Writer experienced in writing engaging, quality and SEO-friendly contents for blogs, articles websites, and more.

I'm skilled in writing articles, content writing, blogging creative writing, as well as research writing.

Check out my profile and follow this link to see my portfolio.

Best regards,

Seun.

5)

Hi James,

I have noticed that you are seeking an SEO blog writer. I'd like to offer you my writing expertise.

As a writer with a creative mind, I'd be thrilled to utilize my skills and reach out to your intended audience! I'm able to write about many different subjects and modify my style of writing to suit.

My blog content is always thoroughly researched, unique and SEO-friendly. As an author, I know the need for original content that shatters Google algorithms and grabs readers' attention at the same simultaneously. My certificate in SEO marketing assures me that I am able to implement SEO concepts that will ensure you are ranked well in Google SERP.

Chapter 5: What's Upwork?

If we take a look at Upwork their profile and company profile, we can say that the company is world's biggest online workspace where over 4 million jobs are advertised each year with a value of 1 billion dollars in total.

Upwork boasts more than 10 million freelancers registered along with 4.5 million registered customers. Customers can conduct interviews and hire freelancers on the Upwork platform.

The company offers a live chat platform. This platform allows customers to hire and find freelancers in very little time. There is no need for geographical or time zone restrictions and clients have access to the world's talent quickly. Employers and the customer do not have to pay any fees.

The freelancers don't need to pay any fee for Upwork's services based on the assignments by the customers. However, 10-20% of the amount paid to the freelancer are collected through the business.

It is possible to say that freelancers do not need to worry about any other thing than this small fee. The funds transfer to freelancers following the period of 6 days using Upwork's escrow service. To make the payments PayPal credit cards or bank accounts may be utilized.

The Upwork platform comes with the ability to use a timesheet application. Its purpose is to keep track of time and capture screenshots when the freelancer is charging to ensure that there is no unfair billing for work that is billed hourly could occur.

Upwork offers a time-tracking application that works on Windows, OSX and Linux. It also offers an app for mobile devices that works with Android along with IOS. In addition, joining to Upwork is totally simple and free of charge. In addition to the excellent services offered by Upwork numerous freelancers and customers use this platform.

Find Jobs and Apply to jobs on Upwork

Making an account on Upwork is an easy job. Anyone who is new to the platform must make an account in Upwork. After completing all step-by-step instructions offered by Upwork the newbie will have their profile fully completed.

A newbie may need to devote 4-5 hours to the process, and after that has to pass a series of tests on the areas in which they have proficiency. Making a profile photo and filling in previous experiences, qualifications and passing the Odesk/Upwork preparation tests, and adding portfolios-all of these are essential to make sure that your profile is that is 100% complete.

In order to find a new job, the newbie must compose a cover letter of his own. Simply copying and pasting the cover letter for job postings is a common practice in Upwork. A well-written cover letter can make a huge difference in helping freelancers who are new to the field get some of the initial clients. Therefore, copying should be avoided.

The cover letter must be specific. If the applicant is a beginner previously worked links, those (if available) must be included. Being a brand new novice should bid on projects that have a low cost. That doesn't mean that after bidding, the beginner may be awarded the project. They may need to wait a while before getting an employment, but both optimism and perseverance should be maintained.

Account suspended by Upwork

Sometimes , accounts get suspended on Upwork. There are several reasons behind this happening.

The majority of the time, bad performance is the primary reason for the suspending an account to ensure the highest standard of work. If a freelancer fails to complete any task or clients find their work to be unacceptable over a lengthy length of time, the freelancer could be branded a an ineffective performer. In addition, poor communication can be regarded as a lack of performance.

Applications that are spammed, using another individual's work as your work, and using of false information, are considered to be typical policy infractions. This is a reason for being able to suspend a freelancer's accounts. Spamming is also in is a violation of the policy. If the user fails to fix the problem and ensures the same violation will not occur the next time, their account is in a restricted state. If a serious violation occurs, the account will be denied reinstatement. The fraud is among the most serious offenses.

Criminal activities such as collusion between accounts, takeovers, and coercion are considered to be serious crimes and are intended to safeguard the user's accounts and financial transactions are stopped.

The rules and guidelines of Upwork must be followed carefully in order to avoid suspension of the account that can result in financial loss.

Everything you need to know about pricing at Upwork

The payment process for Upwork is made through two methods: hourly basis and a fixed-rate. If you are doing hourly work, freelancers must install the Upwork team app which functions as a time tracking tool and as a reviewer for the work diary of the worker. Workers must open the Time Team software's Time Tracker when they begin to work. As per the Upwork rules the client will automatically pay the billable hours. The minimum hourly rate is currently $3.00 USD.

Fixed-price contracts are completely dependent on the client's choice. The contract process is based on the payment terms are set by the client. The issue with this type of payment is the fact that both the quantity and the timing of payment are both dependent on the client. Upwork is not able to provide any guarantees with this method of payment. Therefore, freelancers must be cautious when working with a client using this method of payment.

Payment Methods for Upwork:

PayPal

Payoneer Master Card

Local Bank Transfer

Wire Transfer

It is possible to withdraw money through a variety of ways. Two withdrawal options for distribution funds must be included so that the third method could be a backup option in the event that the first method of funding is not working. Before the beginning of the first contract the withdrawal setup needs to be completed as activation of the withdrawal set takes some time.

Direct payment is a violation of the Upwork regulations. The possibility of using a withdrawal method is contingent upon the country the freelancer is from. ACH as well as Local Funds Transfer are two trusted and recommended options when they are accessible in the country where the freelancer is. In addition, withdrawal via PayPal account is another alternative. The options for withdrawing money are described in Settings >> Get PaidPay Methods

Why do people choose Upwork Freelancing?

A majority of people make a choice to pursue a career because of necessity. However, flexibility is the primary reason to choose freelancing as a profession since you can set your own timetable. They do not have be working for a set period of time because it's done as a full-time salaried job. According to statistics, 78 % of freelancers believe that a freelancer who works regularly earns more than traditional employees in one calendar year, or even less. This means that earning more is a major reason for freelance work.

Since the majority of freelancing jobs are easily found on online platforms, people who work there are more attracted to this career. Platforms such as Upwork make freelancing much simpler than ever before. You can create an account and look for jobs. It is not necessary to search for a job on their own, the platform is an essential instrument in this regard. The Upwork freelancers' working methods is different from the system used by clients.

Upwork is a freelance platform for freelancers.

Utilizing Upwork as a freelancer can be a long-winded procedure. It begins by the creation of an account free. Then , freelancers must create a profile, choose an the hourly rate, and then begin to look for work that match their skills. If he or she finds the job appealing and is interested, then he/she must apply for the position. If he/she is chosen for an interview, and then is hired, then he/she must launch up the Upwork Team Management Application to keep track of the hours they are working. The company guarantees its payments. The freelancers will be paid about 10 days following the conclusion of each week. In the case of fixed-wage, freelancers are paid after six days after Desk's being paid.

Upwork for Clients

The procedure for clients of Upwork is easy. The client must set up profiles and an employment listing that includes an estimate of the hourly rate and time frame. Then, the client can just be waiting for offers to be received. In this scenario, clients do not need to wait for longer. Clients are able to complete another task.

They could conduct a search and then offer the job to freelancers they choose. The next step is to talk with the freelancers, deciding on the one who appears to be most suitable and then granting him/her the task. The Team Management app on Upwork functions as a timer, and will take a picture every 10 minutes. This means that the client does not need to be concerned about whether the freelancer is in work or not. Every now and then, check on whether the progress of the worker.

Alternative Websites of Upwork

The Upwork platform is highly sought-after by freelancers for its top services that cover a broad variety of jobs such as graphics design and computer programming writing articles, SEO and many more. It's among the biggest market place websites worldwide, however it's not the only one in this particular type. There are other websites that offer the same services that Upwork offers. Some of the best alternatives/competitors/similar sites of Upwork are given below.

Freelancer:

Freelancer is among the largest outsourcing, freelance, and crowdsourcing marketplaces across the world. With this platform, the client can employ skilled and proficient freelancers for tasks in the areas of developing, designing software and data entry, as well as writing, etc. The clients need post their requirements and get competitive bids from freelancers.

Fiverr:

Fiverr provides tasks and services that are available to freelancers and businesses. This portal's function is the area of selling and buying gigs or micro-jobs on the internet.

PeoplePerHour:

Peopleperhour is a website similar to Upwork. It offers freelancers to businessmen around the globe. It's much cheaper than staffing companies, employing in-house management overheads as well as working with freelancers, even if they are working remotely.

iFreelance:

iFreelance provides opportunities to customers and bidders using three levels. The levels are simple, silver, and gold. It is unique from other similar websites. It is the most reputable platform for professionals looking for independent freelance work. This is the place that people who are skilled in writing, data entry and web development can connect with entrepreneurs and freelancers with their abilities.

Elance:

Elance is home to 1 million businesses and as many as 3 million freelancers who are registered. On Elance, freelancers, such as writers, designers, and developers are easily found.

ScriptLanes:

Designers, programmers writers, marketers and programmers bid to complete their tasks professionally. This is an easy and most likely to be the most cost-effective site for programming jobs. Scriplane allows entrepreneurs with limited resources to post their work and receive quotations from freelancers.

Guru:

Guru helps businesses find freelance workers for commission work. It provides a safe and secure platform to meet potential clients. It is home to more than 3 million freelancers. This includes software and web writing and translation, finance and management engineering & architecture multimedia, design, and art admin support, and more.

Upwork Review

A variety of aspects can be found in the testimonials of workers of Upwork. If you are able to do legitimate work, you can earn money with Upwork. If an employer/worker examines the profile of the worker or employer properly and then assigns them an opportunity and Upwork gives them a satisfaction, not just for a couple of days, but for longer.

The issue lies in the fact that 10% of payments of freelancers is held on this site. In the general review of users the site's users have legitimate issues. Employers are not always looking for cheap labor. There is a risk that freelancers will not be paid. Some employers are shady and when they have completed the work, they do not make payment for the amount.

Some freelancers deliberately cut corners to ensure they can land an interview. There's always a chance is that your account will be suspended because of an unexpected cause. This is only a problem in fixed-price jobs. An employee can get around this issue by taking time to finish his or her profile to 100%. Both the employee and employer must screen for the other. If this is the case, Upwork is a viable alternative for hiring remote workers or remote work.

Customer Support at Upwork

Upwork provides excellent customer assistance to its clients. It provides its platform safe and secure to ensure that workers can fully trust and be at ease. Its Team Management app gives workers the guarantee of payment. It also allows the clients feel secure that the freelancer is performing their job.

Upwork provides workbooks to new freelancers. Tests on Upwork help freelancers to secure work to their experience and assist clients to find best freelancers for their work.

In the end should any customer have any issues with their account they can get in touch with the support team at Upwork by phone or live chat. They also can be reached via email. Thus, customers do not need to worry about any issue.

Upwork is the biggest and most well-known freelancing website across the globe. Although it does have some disadvantages but its advantages make it the most preferred choice. The system of operation, payment method, testing, and excellent customer support , and more stand it out from other freelancing websites and draw employers as well as the employees.

How can I earn a living by working on Upwork? ($10K Monthly)

It's the most asked most asked question of the year: "Can you make a living from the Upwork platform?". The answer is Yes, it is possible to earn a living from Upwork. Personally, I believe it is entirely feasible to earn more than $10k dollars per month if selected for a job that you are providing services using a traditional payment method.

What is the process? What types of jobs are on Upwork? What's the guarantee that I will not be scammed? Do I have the option of working all hours?

Do you get tired of looking for the right answers for these issues? We've got the answers! You can also read this blog post the overview of your Upwork profile.

What is Upwork, and how Do They Work?

Upwork is a freelancing platform that was previously known as Elance & Odesk. It's an enormous free-standing working space that offers a variety of kinds of independent and business work proposals are available.

It has 12 million freelancers registered and five million clients registered and at the very least, 3 million job opportunities are advertised every year, which is worth a total worth of 1 billion dollars which is a huge amount, making It one of largest marketplaces on earth.

It is simple to join Upwork. It is easy to find a job advertisement first or you find job openings based on your qualifications. Then , you must submit an application with a flawless cover letter. If the client is impressed by your resume and cover letter, he'll reach out to you using the preferred methods of communication, such as skype or email, or Facebook. You and your client will then have a consensus on a shared agreement on time and payment.

When you are done with your work, you are the money. If you aren't sure how to write an effective cover letter? Visit our Best Samples of Upwork Cover Letter. Sometimes , it is the case that you're trying to apply but you're not receiving any responses from your employer. Do you know the reasons for this? The most likely reason is that you're making many mistakes with your proposal. Check out this article to avoid making mistakes in your proposal for upwork.

What is the best way to make a living on Upwork?

In the beginning:

Finding work on Upwork is straightforward because it has job postings for different areas. Although my area includes "Writing and editing" However, you're likely to see a variety in "Programming" as well as "Data Entry" jobs when you know how to complete it. Therefore, you can select the kind of work you'd like.

Secondly:

Being cheated by Upwork is nearly impossible. Upwork operates in a simple and secure way that is "finish your work and please the potential customer". The money is held within Upwork until you have completed the task you promised. If the client tells you that you were ok then the money will be transfered to your account in a timely manner through Upwork following the cutting of their parentsage.

The hourly basis work is more safe than a fixed cost job. You'll be immediate payment for each minute you work. The Upwork desktop time tracker app will track all your work-related activities.

In the initial 500 of your earnings Upwork pays you 20% of the profits. If your earnings exceed $51-9,999, Upwork will take 10% of your earnings. If you manage to charge a customer 10k or more the company will take a 5percent commission. The higher your cost less, the lower your percentage is.

Thirdly:

There is no need to fret about the qualifications or experience you have if you are looking to join Upwork. There is no doubt that freelancers who have a university degree and prior experience are generally preferred by clients however, you can also land an opportunity without it. When I first started my journey my first job, I did not have a degree or any experience in writing content. But, because of my creativity and persistence I made $3k in the very first month. Today, my typical earnings on Upwork is between $10k and $15k, and occasionally $20k when I am working full-time, that's enough to earn a decent life.

Fourthly:

You can be employed full time at Upwork and also part-time. There is no other marketplace that can offer you this kind of the choice of jobs without any qualification or prior experience, full-time job offers, a verified payment method, and nearly a guarantee of receiving a payment from every customer.

In conclusion, based on my own experience, I am able to affirm that it is feasible to make a living through Upwork and earn a good living through it.

How do I create a profile on UpWork?

We've all heard about Upwork and how to sign up. It is the same as making an account on social media. However, simply signing up for an account and filling it out with a random message will not make sense for you.

If you're determined to make an income as freelancer, the very first thing to make is to create a full and appealing profile for a freelancer on Upwork.

The first impression a client gets is their last impression, and your first impression will be derived from the appearance of your profile. As time goes on, I'll show you how to create an attractive profile.

First Sign-up or Register

Let's visit upwork.com/signup and fill in the required fields to fill out the registration form.

2. Make Your Name Your Own

Although it's common to have a legitimate name when conducting business, there are a lot of freelancers still use fake names for their profiles as freelancers.

You are not able to withdraw your funds without having your real name. Don't be embarrassed about your real identity. Don't be afraid to put your authentic name on your profile as a freelancer.

3. Upload a professional image

Do not even think about making use of a selfie, or a bizarre close-up webcam picture for your profile photo. Upload a professional, smiling style portrait.

Make sure you are clean. Dress appropriately. Ask someone else to snap your photo. Don't pay all your attention on the backdrop. Most importantly, smile!

#4 Write a professional Title

Your headline should reflect your title for your job. Therefore, you should be as specific as you can so that it is easier for your clients to understand the work you perform.

Find an area of interest and you'll stand a better chances of being discovered by Upwork Search results.

#5 Write a Professional Summary

Do not describe yourself in third person as if you're telling a story and do not write your profile for freelancers as you would on a corporate site.

The people you are selling to aren't interested your hobbies or ambitions. Keep your personal information to the minimum. This is a profile for freelancers rather than an online dating profile. Make sure to keep the description to a maximum of 200 words.

#6 Describe Your Qualifications and Experience

It is recommended to include a paragraph or so about your credentials and work experience on your resume. Be careful not to boast too much. Don't be the same as this guy.

Also, make use of the "Employment Histories," "Education," as well as the "Other Experiences" sections to give more character to your profile.

#7 Design Some Great Portfolios

UpWork has a distinct section on your profile that is for showing off your portfolio. Use it effectively to showcase your most impressive projects. Details can be found in the Portfolio Part[see Portfolio Part].

Upload a beautiful image, and write a comprehensive description of the project and include the URL of the source.

If you're trying to make your profile on a platform that doesn't offer a portfolio section, you can use a website such as Behance to upload your work . You can then provide links within your freelancer's bio.

#8 Connect Social Networks

UpWork allows you to connect your social media and portfolios to your freelancer's profile.

While the URLs to your profiles on social media aren't visible to your customers it is important to join at least a few of your social accounts to the platform, as it helps UpWorm to understand your needs for a better customized experience. It also allows you to show more relevant job opportunities in the "Find Work" section.

#9 Skill Tests

"The the more pertinent tests that you can pass the more professional your appearance" This is the way it is described by UpWork claims on their website. However, it isn't important how many tests you have passed on UpWork. Customers don't really care about these tests, since these tests don't stand a chance for actual hard work.

#10 Include a Video

UpWork is now allowing you to include a video on your profile as a freelancer. This is a great method to get more attention for your profile. However, it's not required.

#11 Complete Profile Complete

A profile that is 100% complete can increase your chance of landing your first job in the first offer. It's all about confidence. If you have the money, you can purchase some connects in order to bid more on jobs.

I'm sure you've successfully created your account on Upwork.

How do I Get My Upwork Profile Approved?

Today, 90% of freelancers are not getting approval for their profile , and there are reasons for this. The first is that freelancers are growing each day, and so are the work opportunities for freelancers. The most important thing is that false freelancers are entering the market the market without a limit.

Let's be honest and committed to do the job. One suggestion is to keep trying again and repeatedly. In general, you should not like to submit profiles after being rejected initially.

It's possible to have to submit at least 100 multiple times (yes 100 times) until you're accepted. We will follow the steps below to be approved the first time.

#1 Utilize an email address for work. Email Address

Prior to that, you'll be able to utilize your email address similar to that you used to sign-up to Facebook and Twitter. They didn't really care about this option.

However you will notice in the picture below, Upwork specifically asks for an official email address or an official email. This is the initial step in being approved by the automated system for approval of your profile on Upwork. Use an email address that is professional instead of a free and cheap email addresses.

#2. Be specific with your Categories and Skills

Make sure you are specific in your work skills. It is better to position yourself as a top-quality kind of freelancer, such as Roof Designer. If you're looking to join be an operator of data entry but it's not acceptable to Upwork since lots of applications are submitted as Data Entry Worker each day.

3 Select Experiential Levels [Intermediate+3 Select Experience Level [Intermediate+

Many people underestimate their experience, and prefer"Entry" as their "Entry" rather than the "Entry" level (perhaps to keep from obtaining excessive expectations from customers).

But, if you're planning to work from your home, as a self-employed freelancer, and utilize a platform such as Upwork, do not consider yourself an beginner contractor.

This gives an impression that you're not familiar with this and , most likely it's not even clear exactly what you're doing.

4 Your profile 100 100%

The next step is to complete your profile on Upwork 100% including your profile photo and title, overview, rates, portfolio, certificates as well as your employment history. The aim is to demonstrate that you're committed to joining the platform.

There's a good possibility that the human component in the process of approval focuses greatly about your profile's completeness.

In the beginning, make sure you've got a great profile photo. In addition to your profile picture your name is among the most well-known elements on your page. If it's about your rates, don't be cheap. Do not request the minimum acceptable rate, which is $3/hour.

#5 Share Your Experiential

In the section on education Some people write only about their education that they have received. However, it is important to include all your education or even non-formal ones.

In the section on employment history In the employment history section, you must include your experiences regardless of whether they were formal, whether paid or free , that are relevant to the services you offer. It is also essential to add to your employment history certain portfolio items that are relevant to your business.

#6 Refine Your Category

If your preferred abilities and skills aren't over-saturated, you'll be accepted right away.

However, if they don't you'll get the email of Upwork informing you that your application was rejected because your expertise isn't required.

If you've been rejected the first time around, you'll see that you're now allowed to choose more categories than the first time. You can add your categories and subcategories up to the maximum number of categories allowed.

If not, alter the mix of your subcategories and categories. Choose a category closely related to your service.

For instance, if you're a writer of content and have selected "Writing" initially then you can switch the category to "Sales and Marketing" and then select the appropriate subcategories.

#7 What is the reason Upwork refusing to accept my profile?

Demand and supply. It's because there are many freelancers providing specific services, but only a few job openings. This is the reason that many hopeful freelancers with only a basic understanding of research and data entry are turned down.

In recent times, I've also noticed increasing posts on people in the web design and copywriting categories being rejected. The same is true. As more companies offer similar services on Upwork there's always a possibility that the categories might be flagged red.

#8 Keep Resubmitting

Yes, that's work! Resubmit your profile after making certain changes to category fields and the major areas of your profile. Continue to submit your profile until it is accepted.

Create Professional Profile Titles for Upwork

The most professional title you can choose for your upwork profile can raise your chances of winning a job by as high as 90 percent. These examples of professional titles are for those who you're struggling to choose the perfect name for your profile on upwork.

Many freelancers don't know how to include an official title to their profile on upwork to draw the attention of customers. The addition of only the company name can hurt your profile. The title of your profile is an most important element of your success. It will establish your job classification for your customers.

The headlines for freelancers that are professional and the professional title for upwork are among the most popular ways to earn money from freelance. Let's take a look at the top aspects to be successful on upwork.

Professional Title Examples

Be aware that your title should be a reflection of your experience and expertise. Select your title so that the client gets to know the type of work you perform and what area you are have experience in. Your title can be a sort description of skills. Thus, a shrewd title is essential to choose. Avoid using a long title. Instead, a concise and relevant title can be more effective.

Make sure that your title composed of at least 10 characters. All keywords should be included into your title to create a good impression on your. If you're skilled at various types of jobs, you should put your most important job in the first position on your resume. However, we advise you not to utilize more than two kinds of work. Simply highlight your field of interest. You don't have to show your self in the form of an "Entrepreneur" or as a "Jack of all Trades". A simple and concise name will convey that you're dedicated to your job.

Attention from the Client's End

When choosing a title, it's normal to considers the work they perform, what services they provide and what area they are proficient in etc. However, this isn't the best method to select the right title. Instead, think of what your customer can expect from you. Consider how your customers could benefit from your services. This is the method to select a unique name that will attract clients and get them to hire you. Your attention must be devoted to your customer. Be focused on the benefits your client could gain from you.

Make use of a professional title

Professional clients are always looking for professional freelancers. A professional and perfect title will convey a serious impression you give of yourself. Therefore, you should choose an appropriate professional title that is relevant to your job. However, don't choose a vague or complicated title that could cause your customer to switch to the other. Here's an examples of the most appropriate titles for certain occupations to assist you in choosing your own.

01. Professional title to work for Upwork and Data Entry

If you're a freelancer who is an expert at data entry you must identify your specializations prior to writing a professional name. Think about it and then choose a title that is appropriate to the type of service you provide. Here are some examples.

Expert in Data Entry

MS Excel Entry Expert

A Data Arranger, Data Collector and Data Arranger

Pro Data Entry Expert

The first step is to enter data using Excel or SQL

Data Analysis and Data Analysis Mining King

Record Holder and Data Transfer

Web Research and Data Entry Professional

Data Entry Manager

02. Professional Titles for Freelance Writers

There are many different fields to choose from for an author. Therefore, your title should be clear about the kind or writer that you're. It is not enough to utilize "Writer" for your name. If you are a creative writer, you may use

Creative Writer and Copywriter,

Story Writer and Content Specialist

Writer for Kids Entertainment,

Story Writer, E-book Writer

Web Content Writer

Novel Writer and Biography Writer

Writing Expert in Web Content

SEO Article Writer and Provider

Blog and article writer

Pro Email Writer

Content Writer on any subject

Technical Writer, Content Designer and Technical Editor

Content Creator and Creative Writer

Copy Writing Specialist

King of Content and Articles

Professional Word Specialist etc.

In accordance with your preferred styles of writing. If you're an Article Writer , choose:

Pro Article Writer,

Web Page Writer

Blog Writer, etc.

You will be most comfortable.

03. Professional Title Examples for Graphics Designers

If you're an expert at design, select a title that is appropriate to the task. You may use:

Graphics Design Professional

The Artist from the Graphics World

Artist from Art & Design

Graphic Designer and Artist

Design Specialist

Banner Design Expert

Color Design Master

Graphics Media Expert

Graphics Specialist

The King of Graphics Design

Holographic Designing Expert

Professional Color Master

Let's Color Your Dream and something similar to this. Make sure to use a title like this one so that it demonstrates to the world that you are an artist and a designer.

04. Professional Example Titles for Logo Designing

If you are working to design logos only, you are able to utilize

Logo Designing Expert

Create and create logos.

Artist behind Logo Design

A Logo Editor that supports 16M colors

Logo Expert & Text King

Professional Logo Designer

Design Master, Color Enhancer and Logo

Create Your Future Logo

Create logos and brand enhancements with Logo Maker.

2D and 3D Designing Master

King of House Designing

Professional Shop Design

Instrument Designing Expert as your name.

You can also make use of humorous titles, such as:

Logo Guru

Logo Ninja

The King of Logo Maker

Logo Rockstar

to attract clients and increase your the attention of your clients and gain.

05. Professional Title Examples of Web Designer

As a web designer you can refer to the name:

Professional Web Designer. PSD HTML 5. CSS, JS

Expert in Web Expert (PSD converts to HTML)

Web Developer King (Responsive & Dynamic)

Pro Web Design Specialist

Web Designing Master

Pro Web Maker

WordPress Designing Master

Mobile and static web Design

CMS Design with Professional Template

HTML Template Design Expert

Professional Landing Page Design

Professional Web Designer

Responsive Layout Designer for Web

Expert in Responsive Coding

Mobile Web Page Designer

HTML, CSS, Java Script and Photoshop Expert

Web Designing King

Drupal Designer King

Use your personal sense to also attract your customer with your name.

06. Professional Title Examples of Web Developer

Professional Web Developer

PHP Master with 10 Years Experience

Website Back End Developer

Website Database Master

Pro PHP & MySQL Developer

King of Website Design and Developers.

Web Development and CMS Expert

Web Application Developer

Pro Core PHP Developer

Developer of the Landing Page

Ecommerce Website Developer King

Shopify Development Expert

WordPress & Drupal Expert

CMS website and application builder

Reliable Website Designer

Affordable Website Builder

Responsive Web Developer and Coder

Responsive Coder Master

Expert in Mobile Friendly Coding

07. Professional Title on Upwork for SEO Marketer

Professional SEO King

Search Engine Ranking Master

Pro SEO Expert

Google Master and 1st Pare Grantee

Google Bot Expert, Panda, Penguin, Humming Bird

Link Building Expert

Experts in Back-linking

Link King of Wheel Builders

The DA Link Builder Professional

Google Adwords Expert

Google Analytics Guru

1st Page Ranker for SE

Google Search Console and Webmaster Expert

Pro SEO Expert (On-page & Of-page)

Expert in Keyword Research

Long Tail Pro Expert as well as Alexa

Professional Site Auditing King

SEO Checker and ErrorFinder

Google Penalty Recovery Master

08. The Upwork Profile Title is for Digital/SMM Marketer

Digital Marketing Expert

Professional Social Media Marketing

Marketing Booster

Marketing Buzz Creator

Facebook Advertising Master

Pinterest Master and Instagram Master

Social Media King

SMM Engagement Development King

Pages Promoter, Social Media Accounts and Profiles

SMM Product Expert in Advertising

Zero Budget Marketing Expert

09. Professional Title at Upwork for Email Marketer

Professional Expert in Email

Expert in Email Writing and Sending

Pro Mail Chimp Expert

Bulk Email Master

Expert in Marketing Research and Email

Email Sales Expert

Pro Gmail Master and Email

Email Sales Booster

Email Engagement Increased Engagement

10. Professional Title Examples of WordPress Developer

Professional WordPress Designer and Developer

WordPress Theme Integration Expert

WordPress Installation and Development

Pro WordPress Master

WordPress Plugin Expert

WordPress Blogging Theme Expert

Advance WordPress and CMS King

WP Layout Design and Development

Coder in WP PHP Development

The Business Development Team at WP eCommerce

11. Professional Title Examples to Virtual Assistants/VA

Information Entry, VA Workers and VA

Virtual VA Multi-Task Worker

Blogging and the development of a Virtual Assistant

Designing Virtual Assistant

Virtual Assisting in Multi-Tasking Projects

Full-time Virtual expert in maintenance

Full-time Virtual assistant in SEO and Marketing.

12. Professional Title Examples of Mobile Applications Developer

Mobile App Developer

Android Application Developer

ios Application Developer

Mobile App Coder

Professional Mobile App Developer

App Developer in Mobile Platform

13. Professional Title Example to help UI and UX Designers:

Designer of User Interface

Icon along with Front Page Designer

Tab Designer , Layout Designer and Tab Designer

UI as well as UX Professional

Expertise on UI Design and UX Design

14. Professional Title Example of Customer Service

If you're a freelancer who is an expert in customer service, you must choose the particular aspect since there are many kinds that provide customer services. Choose one that you like and choose a title that is appropriate to the services you offer. Here are some examples.

Customer Service Administrator

Live Chat and Support via Phone Representative

Chat, Ticket, Phone Social Support Agent

Customer Service Specialist

Don't choose only "Customer Service" as your title since it's too vague to are aware of.

15. The Upwork Profile Title is for Other Uses

Here are some more names you could apply if your position is compatible with these. They will certainly delight your customer and will give them the impression that you are serious about your job.

Contributing Scribble Supervisor

Director for Alphabet Design and Structure

Professional Blank Page Repairman

Chief Sentence Officer (CSO)

The Keyboard Choreographer, Linguistic Choreographer, and Finger-Dance

Temp-to-Full-Time Prompt Correspondent

Operational Writing Command

Punctuation Team Lead

Word Count Investigator

Fun Titles as well. Works Great

You don't have to be a serious person all the time. There are times when freelancers are praised due to their humorous titles. They're well-known to their clients due to their hilarious titles. They are a reflection of your artistic side. You might hear names such as Social Media Rockstar, Captain of Design, Video Ninja, Copywriting Ninja, Graphics Guru and so on. in certain instances. Some titles are very attractive and operate comparatively faster in comparison to other titles. However, you should use them in a unique way. Be aware that these humorous titles aren't suitable for any profession. These funny titles only if you're employed in a creative career or you are working with children. However, you must make use of your unique name for the job. Do not use a generic name as an address. It can ruin your reputation as a creative worker.

Multitasking Freelancers with Titles

There are numerous freelancers who don't perform only one type of job. They are proficient in a variety of tasks and are looking for jobs of all kinds. If you are a successful candidate, your name could be used to serve a multiple purposes. It has to be able to attract the attention of customers who want these kinds of services you provide. In this case, you have to include all the essential terms of your skills in your one title. However, you should put your main ability first and then add another. Remember that a short title is always superior to an extended one. Don't attempt to include your irrelevant or non-important skills within your name. Keep it to a maximum of 10 words.

Our advice for choosing a suitable job title for freelancers will be helpful to you in your endeavor to freelance. Follow our advice attentively. We hope that you'll be able choose the suitable title that can lead to more opportunities and help you earn more money by freelance. If you've enjoyed our suggestions, do not forget to share our site with other people. We wish you the best of luck in your future career.

Create Portfolio on Upwork [Data Entry]

If you're brand new to freelance and require an example of a portfolio for data entry on Upwork, then this article is for you. Let me start by clearing the confusion: Yes, you can build professional portfolios even if you don't have any prior experience. We'll give you all the tools to create a portfolio that is authentic and professional in comparison to the numerous freelancers who are active in Upwork and freelancer.

Different types of jobs in data entry

There are a variety of jobs that require data entry. If you're new to the field and have no notion of the various the different types of jobs in data entry you can just put it aside and look at the below types of jobs now and you'll learn the various types of work when you complete a couple of projects with the freelancer and upwork.

1. The Image-to-Text Data Entry Project

2. Market Research & Collecting Data

3. Online Formula Filling and Data Entry

4. Converting text to video in a data conversion

Why portfolios are crucial for Freelancers and Upwork

Portfolio informs clients your previous experience and the projects you have worked on for this specific project. If you present your portfolio with professionalism your potential prospects will appreciate it and will offer you the contract. Because the new freelancer can't provide the work history of previous freelancers These portfolios are the only method to give an impression that is positive to customers. Let's find out how.

1. Your profile will be complete. There is no way to attract clients If your portfolio section isn't complete.

2. It boosts your determination and boosts your confidence to be successful in securing jobs.

3. It creates a positive impression to clients and improve the chance to hit to hire.

How Portfolio Section Looks Like

Let's take a look at the data entry portfolio of freelancers and the main types of work.

Single Portfolio Sample from Upwork Freelancer

Let's take a look at an picture of the portfolio of Data Entry of an upwork freelancer. It will display the thumbnail, information entry skills, the project description , and the time of the assignment. This is...

Chapter 6: Sample Cover Letter For An Article Writer

Writing is a profession that is novel. If you're looking to break into this field it is important to determine the source of work. Today, I'm going to describe two different types of job opportunities. One is an organizational platform, and another is a freelancing platform. Upwork is among the top platforms for freelancing around the globe. It has elevated freelance work to the next stage. With the help of Upwork, freelance is no longer just for amateurs. Experts with a professional mindset have taken over the market for freelancers in these times.

This is the reason should you impress your prospective client by your cover letter, you must always think about how writing the most effective one. A generic cover letter is not as effective on Upwork anymore especially if you're seeking an article writer or Content writer job.

Have you composed thousands of cover letters and haven't been able to impress a potential client? Are you slacking off even despite having great writing abilities? What was the problem with your resume cover letter? Do you have any professional tips you didn't know about? Perhaps, you are bored of copying cover letters?

If this is the case for you, then you've come to the right spot. We'll provide you with the most effective example cover letter for an Article Writer/Content writer so that you can craft your own persuasive and intelligent cover letter. Additionally, we'll provide additional details and suggestions for excelling in the professional Article Writing jobs.

Daily Duties to Perform in the capacity of an article writer

Article Writing is not just about writing and submitting your writing to your boss. It has become a major popularity among freelancers due to its writing freedom and reputation as well as the good money.

As a result, customers who use Upwork are always looking for their clients to be involved and knowledgeable. Honesty and punctuality are the main ingredient to succeed in this regard. Plagiarism is totally prohibited in this area since creativity is among the essential traits of an article writer.

There are also the fundamental requirements of freelance Article Writers that include the following:

1. The client receives the article topic list and the directions to the writer from his client.

2. Finding latest and historical references to the subject.

3. Utilizing the internet to search for related information and information.

4. Collecting data and information on the subject.

5. Designing and creating the overall structure that the writer will use with care, and passion.

6. Finding the keyword.

7. Then, arranging the information collected and creating the article.

8. Then, you must send the completed article for the customer.

9. Uploading Articles Online.

Sample 01: Article Writer Cover Letter for Upwork & Freelancer

Dear HR Manager

Good morning.

I am (Write down your name here) and I'm from (Write down your Country's Name). I'd like to announce my candidature to be considered for an Article Writer post in your company that was published a few moments from now on Upwork.

When I first glanced at the job posting and without delay I read the entire advertisement and, after having understood every aspect I was quick to apply for the position. I believe I'm the ideal candidate for your position since you are looking for a skilled and experienced writer to join your team of professionals to make your venture a success.

I feel this certain because of my vast writing experience for more than six years and I have proven my ability to write a variety of articles on a variety of topics.I am well aware of the responsibilities I'll have to perform as a committed and honest employee of the multinational company.

I also have the ability to write quickly on any subject. In previous projects I've written articles about a myriad of subjects such including medieval history, archaeology, medieval history and wildlife, entertainment sociology, world literature, products for hair care review, computers, and more. However, the most important thing is that I don't just create the article, I make sure it's clear and reader comfortable, which is crucial for the project you are working on.

I rely on my expert grasp of MS tools, such as WORD, EXCEL, PowerPoint and the incredible search features using the web platform to create a 100 100% clients' happiness merger.I also have a fast typing speed and ability to read.

My academic background has also made me succeed in this area. I am a graduate in Arts and Sciences with English literature as a graduation discipline from the university of .... 2016 2016. (Write your personal university and the year of graduation here).

I am confident that if I am hired I will be working for more than 60 hours per week to make your venture succeed in a short amount of time.

I'd love to get in touch with you soon. Contact me by Email or Skype because I'm always available.

Thank you.

Tips for Writing a Killer Cover Letter for Article Writer:

If you've looked over our sample of cover letters below you might have noticed some tips already. However, let's review the most important tips once more.

1. Greet in a Professional Approach: Dear Hiring Manager/ Dear Potential Client etc.

2. Don't try to write your cover letter without having read the job title and description carefully.

3. Let your client know that you are able to perform your duties the job described in his description without difficulty.

4. Straight to the issue without slashing off additional words.

5. Be sure to mention your education achievements and your previous experiences.

6. Don't bore your customer with a plethora of promises.

7. Your Working Hours Per Week

8. The most convenient contact options

9. Formal goodbye.

Sample 02: Article Writer Cover Letter for Organization

In this scenario, you have to adhere to some standard rules and guidelines to write your letter of cover. A brief basic, but efficient cover letter is needed at this point. Thus, you need to keep it short and use only the information that is required as the client demands. the following format of an organizational job cover letter:

1. Your Name:

2. Your Address:

3. Your email address:

4. Your phone:

Employer's Name:

Employer's Address:

The date is 01-01-(in the year of this)

Dear [Client NameDear [Client Name]

1st Para:

The name of the job that you're applying to or the job source you are applying for and your personal interest.

2nd Para:

Your work experience, skills education, and your success overview,

3rd Para:

The goal of this project is and your assurance of transparency, integrity, process of work and timing schedule

4th Para:

Thank you client, Communication Medias, ready to collaborate,

Thank you very much.

[Your Name]

Cover Letter Example to be used for Virtual Assistant (VA)

Are you in search of the perfect cover letter template for Virtual Assistant that will impress your customer? We're here to assist you with this. There is a wealth of secrets and requirements for creating a cover letter to apply for the position of Virtual Assistant here.

We will help you to get a better understanding of Virtual Assistant (VA) and how to write an effective Cover Letter for it. We'll provide two kinds of cover letters. One is for the Upwork and Freelancing platform and the other designed for an individual business. I would like you to go through the entire article and download Upwork's overview sample.

The reason why your cover letter is important

In the beginning, what is the reason you should be mindful of writing a cover letter. The cover letter you write is probably the primary factor to grab your client's focus. Your prospective employer won't be able to see your cover letter or your resume or any of your other work in the beginning. The cover letter you write is the one which your recruiter will look at first. Now that you know, your cover letter is the first impression on your customers. This is why you need to write it in as to serve as a bridge between you and the position you're hoping to achieve.

What is Virtual Assistant is it?

A few people begin writing their cover letters and do not even know about Virtual Assistant properly. In the end, they don't get the job they want. It is important to be aware of the definition of VA is also known as Virtual Assistant is and what kind of work they perform before you write a cover note to apply for the position of Virtual Assistant. Therefore, let's gather some understanding of Virtual Assistant before starting with the cover letter.

Virtual Assistant plays a very vital role for any company because they offer clerical and operational support. However, they do not communicate with their customers directly. Instead, they assist their customers via the internet or another ways of communication. In general, when entrepreneurs are busy, but need to complete their day-to-day tasks They appoint

Virtual Assistants to complete the work on behalf of them. Virtual Assistants assist them in manage the strategic actions on the internet. They usually perform the following for recruiters-

* Scheduling Appointments

* Attending phone calls

* Create Presentation

* Customer Service

* Controlling email

* Travel arrangements

* Update Websites frequently

* Database Update

* Content Writing

* Doing Errands

* Assisting in recruiting

* Computer skills

* Skills for organizing

* Plan

* Effective communication

* Excellent interpersonal skills

* Self-motivation

* Creativity and determination

* Problem-solving orientation

• Diplomacy, tact and respect

* Time management, deadline planning.

Tips for Writing a Killer Cover Letter for Virtual Assistant

You now know what the Virtual Assistant is and what sort of job they perform. Let's get started with our cover letter to apply for the position of Virtual Assistant. Here are some guidelines for writing a great simple, well-written and powerful cover letter that will grab the attention of readers that will aid you in reaching your goal.

1. Find out about your client's needs:

Before writing your cover letter, read the job advertisement carefully. Also, conduct research about your prospective employer. Determine the skills and performance that your customer wants from the employee. This will allow you to understand the exact requirements your client has from you. and convince the reader of your letter of introduction that you are the sole person your client requires to complete his job.

2. Formatting:

Your cover letter needs to be formatted in a consistent format. A good cover letter is composed of three elements: a formal salutation, an attractive introduction, a brief description of your personality and a positive conclusion with your signature. Therefore, you should try to adhere to the same format when writing a cover letter.

3. Header:

Make sure to include your full name with your contact phone number and address in in a clever manner.

4. Introductory Paragraph

In the introduction paragraph, be sure to mention the purpose for writing, which is the title of your job and include a the reference to the job posting. Then, you should introduce your client to them by stating your academic and professional qualifications.

5. Development:

In the following paragraph, develop your reasoning in a clear manner about why you're right for the position. Your experience and your confidence in your job. Your reader should believe that you enjoy the work of a virtual assistant with all your heart.

6. Conclusion Paragraph:

In the closing paragraph, express your positive outlook and describe your availability. You can ending with the expectation of a subsequent contact. Make sure to follow it up with your signature.

This is the correct way to compose a standard cover letter to apply for the post of Virtual Assistant. If you're still confused and have a difficulties in creating a compelling cover letter, check out the sample below of a fantastic cover letter for the position in the field of Virtual Assistant. You'll definitely be able create a cover letter of standard format your self. I hope you can take you to where you want to go. Best wishes to you.

Sample 01: Cover Letter Template for Upwork

Thank you Heylon, I am your dearest. Heylon,

We wish you a wonderful day.

I've read the job posting and came to learn that you're searching for a reliable Virtual Assistant to work for your business. Because it's a major passion of mine to work as a virtual assistant, I do not want to miss the opportunity , so I'm apply for the position. As a post graduate in ICT and having many years of experience, I consider myself as the best trustworthy person to do the job.

I have been working as freelancer and an Assistant Virtual for the past five years. This has helped me become more proficient in my job. I have a stunning convincing ability to deal with clients via internet or by phone. Additionally, I can deliver a presentations in a brief time and in a highly effective manner. For my professional needs, I have a wonderful arrangement of computer components with an internet connection that is strong as well as a fixed landline phone printer, fax machine, and more. inside your home, in a quiet pin drop space that is suitable for such a use. This allows me to work anytime of the day or night wearing my jeans. I am in a great surroundings and love the variety of tasks that the job provides every single day.

You can therefore be confident in me to complete any task as a virtual Assistant. I'm ready to assist you up to 60 per day. I'm impatiently waiting to hear from you. I'm available at all times via my Skype and email.

Thank you so much for taking the time to read the letter.

Saxena

Sample 02: Cover Letter for Virtual Assistant Letter Example for Organization

When you create a cover letter in response to your client's job advertisement You must follow certain traditional guidelines. While this isn't a must, doing your best to show respect is always the best. Let's be respectful.

Date: 3 July 2011.

From:

1. "Mr. Guilbert Saxena

2. 2012 Western Lane, Los Angeles, 125-402-011

3. Guilbert120@example.com To:

1. The Mr. Robert Heylon,

2. New Street, 1240 Holy Yard, NY 201456

Re for to fill in the Post of Virtual Assistant.

Cover Letter Example for Web Developer

Looking for a professional upwork cover letter format for web developer? Then, don't worry. You'll find plenty of helpful tips that will assist you in achieve your goal. I hope this article can end your search for a proposal for upwork example for web developer. I would like to ask that you read the entire article to the at the end.

However, the writing of a cover letter shouldn't require you to write the format that you want to use for it. Keep an eye on the way your resume is going to reflect your skills, personality and proficiency in your work. The client will evaluate you based on your writing in the cover letter. Therefore, you should compose your upwork cover letter that is effective and attractive manner. It must be able to grab the attention to your customer right from the first time they read it. If you require Screening Questions and Answer for Upwork, click the link.

In this article, we will talk the process of writing an upwork cover letter to promote web development, it's important to be aware of the key words that are frequently used when it comes to web development as well as web development prior to beginning writing the letter of introduction. Web development, as we all know isn't just a field for short. It is more of an orientation for their work in developing and creating an online delegate site for the purpose of promoting their services to the world. It is also referred to as the "World World Wide Internet" development.

A different kind of web Developers is another one that are dedicated to SEO and Graphics development of various intranets for a business. Intranet is an additional crucial term used here to refer to the private network of an individual that is employed within his specific area of. We'll discuss the main aspects of web development near the conclusion of this article. in the meantime we will look at an example of a web developer's cover letter:

Must! Study Before Making Proposals

Let's look at what is the Web Development. It encompasses a range of work that can be categorized as Web Development. Its range is quite large. In reality, Web development can range from the static simple web page with a few words, to the largest array of web-based internet-based applications, electronic business, and social networking services .Web web-based applications are often referred to by the name of Web App. This isn't the end of the story. A variety of more complex and inclusive tasks are also covered in Web Development. There are many terms that you may have heard of the terms: client liaison web engineering, client-side or server-side scripting, web content creation, development of e-commerce security configuration for the web server, and network configuration. All of these are covered in Web Development.

It's just the basic idea that is Web Development. In reality, Web Development means quite differently from the professional web developers. For them, Web Development means the non-design elements of developing web sites which includes writing, marking up, and programming.

For the present, to professionals, Web Development means mainly the creation the design, direction and development of Content Management Systems or CMS. CMS, also known as contents management systems, CMS can be developed from an open source project, proprietary, or graze. CMS could be a brand new term to you.

There's nothing to be worried about. I'll go over it with you. It is a term used to describe a system that acts as a middleware that connects both the databases and users via the browser. Now, you might be curious about the benefits of CMS. CMS.

So, let me explain the concept in your own words. There are many people who aren't technical and do not have any technical expertise in their own lives, but want to design, build or alter their website site. In this case, CMS is a wonderful solution for those who aren't tech-savvy. It lets them improve their websites according to their requirements.

Sample 01 Proposal for Upwork Sample for Web Developer

Dear Hiring Manager

I wish you a very happy day!

In response to your recent job advertisement on Upwork, I'm here to apply for the Web Developer job. I have a solid experience for Web Developer, along with my formal studies of Computer Science and Technology. My work experience and academic training have provided me with exceptional and technical abilities. In addition, I possess the ability to create a unique design that is unique. I believe these attributes distinguish me from the other contestants.

I'd like to tell you that I am extremely skilled in HTML, CSS, and JavaScrip since I have vast experience with it. However, I am always keen to keep learning and making my abilities sharper each time I have the opportunity.

Beyond that I have a strong enthusiasm for mobile technology and software technology too. I've had the pleasure of working with a number of mobile-related companies and loved working with them quite a bit. They are impressed with my enthusiasm, dedication and endurance.

Why I believe me to be the most qualified candidate and an excellent contribution to your endeavor. My profile, portfolio , and work history are all included to your consideration to help you appreciate my abilities.

Thank you for your time in to read the letter. I look at receiving your feedback for the next procedures.

Thank you for your kind words.

Your Name.

4 important facts you must keep in mind

When you are done you've aware the fact that Web Development is not any simple thing that everyone could accomplish. If you're planning to write a cover letter, you should be mindful of these issues in your head. It is also important to do certain things with great diligence.

Firstly:

Learn how to utilize the scripting or authoring language to create a website. These languages will form the foundation of your website. Therefore, you won't have the option of making the wrong thing there.

Secondly:

It is important to follow the correct method of writing, designing , and editing the content of your website. If you're asking others do the job, then you should direct them in a correctly to ensure that the content of the page can be effective and coherent to the purpose you are trying to achieve.

Thirdly:

It is essential to identify the issues after the first time you touch them up and fix them right away. It is possible to assist in as well by identifying the errors through conducting tests or by analyzing feedback from the user.

Fourthly:

It is essential to be aware of how to convert an element to web-friendly formats compatible. The majority of these components are either graphic or written or video formats. You will need convert these formats to web-based formats.

The last but not last:

It is recommended to check out the cover letter sample below which will assist you in learning how to compose personal cover letters to jobs that require upwork. You'll learn the structure of creating a cover letter by looking at these examples. However, cutting or copy paste won't always yield the desired results, you're aware. Make use of your own words and express your imagination using your own words, following the format established and you'll be able to achieve the desired outcome.

Follow these guidelines with extreme attention and I guarantee you'll be able to compose an impressive cover letter yourself.

Web Developer Job Sample Job Posting 01:

Cover Letter Example for WordPress Developer

Are you an WordPress designer or developer? If you're in search of the most impressive and captivating cover letter to promote you WordPress Development, you are at the right spot since I'll provide several professional cover letter examples for WordPress developers.

It is possible to use it on freelancer, upwork and other marketplaces for freelancers. If you're still unable to choose a particular platform for marketing freelancing then this article is for you: Upwork or Freelancer, which is the better choice?

A standard cover letter serves the purpose of presenting your capabilities to the customer. It is therefore important to create your cover letter attractive with all formalities in place and including all the essential details.

In the modern age there are many who work with different types of freelance jobs. WordPress is among them. It's also interesting that there are many job applicants who apply to WordPress without knowing the basics of what WordPress actually means and what it requires. If you know the basics of WordPress it's difficult to write an impressive and effective letter of introduction for Upwork.

It is important to be aware of the basics of what WordPress is. In essence, it's an open source, online website-building tool developed in PHP. There's hardly a prominent business in the world today that doesn't use WordPress to promote their business on the World Wide Web. WordPress is the best way to showcase your products to the general public. It's probably the easiest and most popular blog and website content management system , now referred to as CMS. A multitude of businesses, including well-known blogs and news media and music sites Fortune 500 companies and celebrities use WordPress to fulfill their needs. In a nutshell, they have to be using it. If you don't know how to write a cover Letter, click the link.

Now, if you're feeling that you could be a good candidate working on WordPress tasks, ensure you're aware of how to complete these tasks successfully prior to sending a cover letter to Upwork.

Here's a list of examples and guidelines to write an effective cover letter.

The Sample 1: WordPress Cover Letter for Upwork and Freelancer

Hello,

Let's get straight to the main point. I discovered that you require a WordPress E-commerce site with a beautiful front-end design and completely safe background calculation. Based on the description you provided you'll need to get the job accomplished quickly and on budget-friendly prices. In addition, you're not planning to use your credit card to purchase plugins or themes for WordPress.

The requirements you have set out are crystal evident to me. I'm applying because I fulfill all the criteria that you're looking for. I've been an wordpress designer and developer for over 10 years, and I am aware of the aspects of WordPress development and customizing.

Ecommerce site must be completely secure. This is my first guarantee in this endeavor. Furthermore I will be available to you for any type of modifications and edits in the future. In some cases, my five years back clients are looking for me until this day only due to my services.

I am a lover of communicating. I enjoy staying close to my clients throughout the day so that they are able to reach me at whenever they need me. I'm easy to make use of any type of computer or mobile device to stay in touch to you.

I'm in search of specific requirements documents of your website to allow me to begin working on it immediately. If you would like to talk with me about any type of advice or information I am available at any time. I look to hear from you soon.

Yours

Devid Marthin

The Sample 2: WordPress Cover Letter for Organization

In this scenario, you have to adhere to the traditional guidelines and formats in your covering letter. A brief and simple, yet effective cover letter is necessary during this phase. Thus, you need to keep your cover letter concise and contain only the essential information the way your client would like it. the below format for the cover letter:

1. Your Name:

2. Your Address:

3. Your email address is:

4. Your phone:

Employer's Name:

Employer's Address:

Datum: 01-01-(in the year of this)

Dear [Client NameDear [Client Name]

1st Para:

The name of the job that you're applying for or the job source you are applying for and your personal interest.

2nd Para:

Your abilities, experience at work as well as your education and achievement overview.

3rd Para:

Your objective in this project is to provide sincerity, integrity, and time-frame.

4th Para: Thank you to the client, the communication medias and is ready to work.

Thank you for your consideration.

[Your Name]

Cover Letter Example for Graphic Designers

This sample upwork proposal graphic designer is a kind as a ticket for the dream freelance job. A well-written cover letter is the most important factor to entering your fantasies of freelance. If you're creating an upwork cover letter that is graphic it is essential to show your imagination through the design and the words in your cover letter since you are bidding on a unique job.

Let's look at the top Upwork cover letter examples for graphic designers to help you prepare the best way to write your own proposal for Upwork. The employer must have an idea of your skills and confidence through your application letter. Therefore, you must be aware of crafting a powerful cover letter for Graphic Designing. Also, you can look up the Upwork Overview Samples

Cover Letter for Graphic Design Secret Tips?

Are you looking for secrets to writing an amazing cover letter with graphic design? That's right, create attractive responses to the screening questions you ask your prospective clients. These questions are first asked at the end of your client's request and then in your cover letter. If you fail to provide satisfactory answers then the recruiter will not go towards your resume. We'll give you every strategy to ensure that your customer will be happy and will call you to schedule an interview. Use our methods to make your cover letter stand out from other ones.

Graphic Design in Full

Before you can understand the guidelines for creating a cover letter specifically to be used by a Graphic Designer you must know at the beginning the meaning of Graphic Design actually means to understand what the recruiter is looking for from you.

It's ok, Graphic Designing actually indicates communicating your message or thoughts by using graphic images and visual media. Each Graphic Designing project will tell an engaging story using images for the aim of promoting goods activities, ideas, or communicating. Also, it involves using HTML codes for e-mail announcements and invitations, experience making brochures, advertisements, and newsletters. Strong imagination and proficiency with a range of graphic design tools.

When you're applying for a position your cover letter will be the most crucial part of the interview process. This is why you should make use of your creative skills as a designer in making a cover letter. Create your cover letter in an appealing and clever manner to ensure that the person you are contacting is impressed at first sight. Let's look at two examples of a successful cover letter for a Graphic Designer.

Sample 01: Cover Letter for Upwork Example for Graphic Designers

Dear Mr, Clare

I've learned through your circular that your graphic department requires a professional designer who has demonstrated talent and technical expertise as well as a keen desire to keep learning and be successful. As a result, I'm offering myself to fill the post that is currently vacant. I have an excellent experience using web design software as well as a design software. I've been able to satisfy the majority of my customers with my creative skills.

Designing graphics is an art form through which it is possible to communicate a multitude of meanings about it. It provides a variety of extra perspectives to a simple creation. I'm ready to supply various types of graphics, including banners, logos, banners cartoons, 3D images and so on.

Please take into consideration the following abilities for me to be a potential candidate:

1. An advanced Master in Fine Arts with Bachelor degree in the subject of Graphic Designing.

2. Thesis on advertising photos for a the cultural program.

3. Expertise in Adobe Illustrator, Adobe Photoshop, Adobe Image Ready, CSS, Word Press, Quark Xpress web etc.

4. Amazing performance in team management as well as Customer Service.

5. Agility in visual strategy layout design and in electronic

6. Three years of expertise in the field of Graphic Designing and animation software.

7. Design-driven passion and innovative work.

Additionally there are a lot of online graphic works that I've done over the last few years. I've attached the URL to these portfolios which will give you a better impression of my talent. My academic and professional experience demonstrate the quality for my works. I am convinced that I will be qualified to contribute to your venture.

You can also look over my resume here. Contact me if you have any concerns or questions you want to know about me. I'm always available via my skype and email.

Thank you for your consideration. I'm waiting for your reply to continue the steps.

Yours sincerely

Bardoon

Example 02: Graphic Design Cover Letter Example to help with Organization

In this scenario, you have to follow a few traditional guidelines and formats in your covering letter. In general, a brief basic, but efficient cover letter is needed during this phase. Therefore, you should keep your cover letter short and include only the information that is required as the client demands. the following format of the cover letter:

1. Your Name:

2. Mailing Address:

3. Your email address is:

4. Your phone:

Employer's Name:

Employer's Address:

Datum: 01-01-(in this calendar year)

Dear [Client NameDear [Client Name]

1st Para:

The name of the job you are applying for, your job source, your passion and so on.

2nd Para:

Your abilities, experience at work educational background, and your success overview.

3rd Para:

The goal of this project is your assurance integrity, honesty, process and schedule.

4th Para:

Thank you to the client, and thanks for the Communication Medias, waiting to get to work.

Thank you for your consideration.

[Your Name]

What to write the Most Effective Graphic Cover Letter for Design

Let's now learn on how to write a memorable and persuasive cover letter for Graphic Design.

01. Personalize your letter

Your letter should be lively to ensure that throughout the letter the reader can feel your presence. It is important to make an appearance that is formal in your letter. So. Your cover letter should be written so that you present yourself as a professional.

02 Particular Address

It is always best to speak directly with your recruiter. It is essential to find out who actually is hiring you. Do not address your letter the address as "To whom it is appropriate" or something similar to that. In the end, it's a typical address. Therefore, to make your cover letter stand out, you must stay clear of these typical addresses. Do your homework to find out the name of your prospective employer and how to write them a specific letter.

03. Consistently written

Keep your writing consistent beginning with the first line through the final. It is not possible to alter your style based on your desires. It could seriously harm your letter. Make sure you choose your design carefully and present yourself in a coherent manner and displaying the best qualities you can offer for the task.

04. Highlight your skills

In your letter, it is important to be sure to highlight your expertise, professional experience and academic credentials. Make sure to convince your reader of how much you cherish your work and are enjoying the process. Let your design passion shine through.

05. Regarding Portfolio

If you want to talk about your portfolios, you don't have to include it directly in the cover letters. Instead, you could present your portfolios you've put into reassurance that your potential employer of your professionalism and knowledge. If you have an online portfolio, include the URL with your resume cover letter. This will catch the attention of your prospective employer.

06. Recheck

After you've written your letter of cover, make sure to check your cover letter over and repeatedly. It will help you figure mistakes and increase the strength of your words by editing. In fact, it's a great practice to review your letter prior to pressing the submit button.

07. Designing

To write a cover note in the field of Graphic Design, the design of the cover letter itself is vitally important. Therefore, you must design your words and your letter with a stylish appearance in order that your letter conveys the impression that it's a cover design letter.

08. Give yourself time

Do not rush to write an effective cover letter. You must take your time in order to make your cover letter unique and impressive. You should think about what you would like to emphasize, create an outline, then write it in a careful manner and then edit it to improve and edit.

You can see that these examples are all great ways to write a compelling cover letter to get work Graphic Design. Follow these guidelines attentively and you'll be able write an impressive covering letter which will boost your company fortune.

Chapter 7: Profile Overview Sample For Virtual Assistant (Va)

Are you just starting out in upwork and want to join as a virtual assistant? Are you not receiving enough responses from your clients? You must make your profile more appealing as a virtual assistant.

When you're presenting yourself as an expert Virtual Assistant it is essential to impress your customer by providing an overview. It is your overview that is most crucial element of your profile clients take very seriously. Therefore, stay with us for tips on how to create a an amazing overview of your work to be a virtual Assistant in order to please your customer.

Steps to Create a Gorgeous Upwork Overview of Virtual Assistant

It's quite easy to create a stunning overview using a Virtual Assistant. It's all you have to do is follow the steps listed below.

First Impression is the Last Impression:

It's a well-known, wise and helpful saying says your first impression will be your final impression.

Therefore, you should apply the same technique to your advantage here too. Your client will be impressed by your first impressions. Let your client know that you're the ideal virtual Assistant for him with your first sentence.

Make sure you are professional.

Your client will believe you are an experienced Virtual Assistant with your professional voice. Be aware that you are not allowed to make use of any salutation in this speech. Overview is just a brief statement of yours describing your expertise. There is no one to whom you are speaking in this article. Therefore, avoid using any salutation, such as: Dear sir hello, hi, hi or any other wish such as good day or good night, etc.

Make use of your own voice:

Everyone hates copying when you're required to introduce yourself. Use your own voice using only the most authentic and authentic information to earn the trust of your clients.

You will be able to present yourself as an assistant virtualized Only:

It is not necessary to include the other skills you do not have in your summary. Instead, concentrate on your expertise being a virtual assistant. It will make the client believe that you're an expert in that area only and only.

Write a clear overview:

It's true that nobody enjoys an interminable and boring piece of writing. If they see your lengthy outline, your reader will keep you from the pleasure of it. Therefore, the best way to go is to provide a short and straight-forward overview, not getting bogged down.

Your Reason for Being chosen:

It is crucial convincing your customer that they should choose you over the many Virtual Assistant candidates for the job. Be sure to explain in your brief the reason why your client should choose you.

Revise and correct:

There is no way to make a mistake in your summary. Also, make sure to make sure you revise the overview after having completed it, and make sure you correct any mistakes you've made. You can improve your presentation to give it more power.

A Sample of the Upwork Overview of Virtual Assistant

If you are still having doubts when writing your summary in the context of Virtual Assistant look up on the following example. It can help you to write your own outline:

I am a skilled self-motivated Virtual Assistant with a high level of skill and experience that spans six years. I have an extensive understanding of virtual functions since I've conducted some research in connection with my studies in Virtual Science. I've been working for an internationally renowned Multi- International Company as an Assistant Virtual for the past five years. Currently, I run a successful web site of my own.

I am passionate for being a virtual Assistant. I am always awake to be aware of the most recent and up-to-date materials. I do my best to enhance my skills and perform my job. In addition, I possess an impressive and persuasive ability to handle any kind of consumer.

To top it off, I've created a personal space complete with all types of virtual-purpose elements such as a high-end computer, reliable internet connection, land-line phone, fax and printer, to ensure 24 hour accessibility to my customers, which is essential for a virtual Assistant.

In addition, I am an the expert on

Scheduling appointments

Making Presentations

Serving Customers

Helping the rude customers quickly

Travel management

Skills in Organization

Updating Database

Problem Solving and Orientation

Planning

Writing Content

Profile Overview Example for Web Developer

Download the Profile Overview sample of web developers which will assist you in make the most effective profile on Upwork for web developer that will draw your clients. Web developers' job is to experiment with web basics in order to build World Wide Web applications.

Web developers who are freelance have experience in creating applications using the client-server model such as Python, HTML, JavaScript, PHP, CSS, C#; the clients for their own benefit are obliged to provide tasks to these freelancers. However when the summary of your profile isn't convincing enough, clients may not select you. You must convince your client that you have expertise in web development. You you must also give your client believe that you're not the identical to the other web developers.

What Should You Write About in your Web Developer's Overview

It is possible to take a project to completion with fewer mistakes and at the highest level of potential and with great transparency and in a totally distinctive manner. Inform your employer that you are a master of problem-solving strategies and that you appreciate your time. Additionally, you want to be honest. Remember that an error in the design of your work can prevent the entire webpage from running, which is why you need to keep an eye on the vulture. If you hold a bachelor's degree or Master's Degree in Computer Engineering or Software Engineering make sure to mention this in your overview of your profile as it increases the demand of your profile and the client will not hesitate or have any hesitation in hiring you.

Technical Section of Your Profile Summary

If you don't have these qualifications Do not fret. Give them a few examples of professionally designed websites, its needs, reviews, and the popularity with the general public. Additionally, include your long-term expertise in this area so clients understand that you're not new and that working with you on the project will not result in any losses. The most important thing is to show your uniqueness by being honest and avoid using your work for plagiarism. Make sure that you show that the quality of work is not the same with others, and it's very satisfying since all clients have been satisfied with your work.

The overview of your profile at Upwork for web developer needs to be brief, clean impressive, and informative. don't beat over the head. Make sure you are clear and confident when writing the summary. If you've developed a few guidelines that can aid you in creating a an exciting new venture with a lot of money I'd like to share with you an example of a an overview of a profile for web developers.

Sample 01: Overview of Upwork Profile A Sample Web Developer

Hello!

Before discussing the qualifications and skills of professionals I'd be pleased to introduce myself.

I'm Devid Buffelo and I am from the United States. Making web development an occupation not only fills my wallet, but also my heart since it has been my love since the time I was in my teens.

I believe that people should pursue things that they are proficient in or where their heart is. This is why I decided to work as a web development freelance as my profession since I'm confident in this field and that I'm honest and am not intimidated by difficult work.

I've graduated at The University of (university name. If not, please take the exam) in Computer Science Engineering and I have had many classes on modern web design from renowned institutions. My academic background helped me to succeed in this field, and my education in this field have made me an expert in this field.

I am extremely proficient using both Swift and Objective C.I also understand the usage of Kotlin and Java for iPhone, iPod, Android and Tablet. I've created a number of websites to make them more efficient in their search engine and provide user interfaces that are easier to use.

Recently, I've designed an online platform that assists its users learn the best ways to use their free time . This the website has been very well-known among students. The title of the website is (include the name of the site If not, please pass).The mobile app for the website was created by me, and it is rated with been given a 4.4 rating on Google Play store.

This is only one of my successes as a web developer freelance. I am certain that if I am hired I can show you with many projects that have been successful with little effort from your part.

I will give you a refund guarantee and guarantee you that you won't regret hiring me.

Thank you.

Sample 02: Overview of the Upwork Profile Example for Web Developer

Hello,

This can be (write on your paper your initials).

I am an experienced back-end web developer and have been in this area for seven years.

I hold a bachelor's degree with a major in Software Engineering from the university of (write down the name of the university you attended and if it doesn't or none, just go through) as well as a course for graphic design.

I've already earned an impressive amount of fame by creating a number of famous websites. Recently one of my websites have received numerous responses from clients. Below is an attachment (mention the work you've done).

I have a solid understanding of graphic design and programming. my work is not just beautiful but also incorporates videos, graphics and audio. I'm also proficient in ways to solve problems and am familiar with the computer language like Python, PHP, CSS, XML, HTML, HTML5, SQL, JavaScript and multimedia publishing tools such as Flash as well as Photoshop.

Additionally the fact that my websites are SEO-friendly because they has never failed to please the customers. In addition, I keep myself current with the latest technologies and their applications as well as new tools and computer languages to ensure I can provide the best I can to my customers. I am a firm believer in the power of hardship, and hiring me will not be a mistake.

Thank you.

Profile Overview Template for WordPress Developers

If you're in the market for an expert overview of upwork for a WordPress developer This article will satisfy the need. I'll offer not just an overview sample , but also essential things to keep in mind when creating a wordpress profile for a designer.

Today, being professional freelancers through Upwork has become extremely well-known. There are many kinds of freelance jobs on the market, WordPress Designing & Developing is among the most sought-after and coveted one.

Here is the top Upwork Overview Template of WordPress Designer & Developer to make your prospective clients awestruck. Are you aware of what a client expects from a freelancer he has hired?

Demands from Clients

The needs of the client are straightforward however, they are difficult because their demands are based on -

High-Quality Work

Creativity

Uniqueness

Punctuality

Methods for solving problems

Honesty

Transparency

Experience

The value of money

Now that you have a better understanding of what the needs of your customer, let's begin to create your Upwork Profile Overview . you are a WordPress Designer and Developer.

Example 01: Overview of the Upwork Profile for WordPress Developers

Hello,

My name is (write down your name here).).

I've been an experienced CSS, Angular and WordPress developer for over 7 years. I also have gained recognition and fame as a Front-end Developer.

There are a lot of freelancing Web as well as WordPress developers in the market, I rate myself the best, as during my career, I have never had a single unhappy client.

I hold a Bachelor's Degree in Computer Science Engineering from The University of (your university's name, if you don't then you must pass.)

I have a vast knowledge of creating web-based applications using a variety contemporary technologies. I'm also extremely proficient in managing websites and mobile applications as I'm an expert making use of WordPress WooCommerce PHP as well as HTML/CSS. My main focus is on creating quality SEO-friendly modules and high-quality code.

As I host my own web hosting account I will be capable of showing you the working progress at any time that you'd like.

Other professional abilities include:

Utilization of PSD2HTML

Utilization of JQuery

Web Designing talent

Ability to solve problems

Rapid response

UX and UI design

Supervising and monitoring

I believe in hard-working and integrity. I am always looking forward to developing long-term professional connections with my clients to ensure that each project is profitable. If you decide to hire me, I will promise you that you'll not regret it.

Important Tips:

Your profile must be to the point and concise. While the majority of clients prefer experienced profiles but if you're an experienced professional experience, then it doesn't matter as much. This is why it's essential to state your expertise and experience as an WordPress Developer.

Do not provide false information:

since your customer is likely to verify your claims prior to hiring as they are most likely to check your claims before hiring. Look over this sample overview of your profile and create your own description of your profile.

Summary:

This sample overview of your profile serves as a reference to help you ensure that you create the most effective profile overview by yourself. Don't use this sample to use as your main description of your profile because it's an example of a template.

Best of luck!

Profile Overview Example for Graphic Designers

This sample profile overview for Upwork for graphic designers is vital because a great profile overview is extremely needed for jobs on Upwork in the ever-changing world of graphic design.

A stunning overview and the recruiter feels compelled to take you on regardless. However, before you can do that you must gain experience by reading through job advertisements and what client can expect of you prior to accepting any job. In the beginning, as graphic designers, you must create a profile image that is clear, yet professional in its nature.

You could add your personal personality to the profile picture to impress your clients and it could be considered your first impression of you. However, be sure to avoid any exaggeration, and keep it easy to look beautiful. You can then add the essential capabilities that are essential to be successful in this job.

They include:

Creativity and imagination are the powerhouses that can unleash creativity

Utilization of Adobe illustrator

Photoshop InDesign and Print Design Print Design, Photoshop, Design

Adobe Creative Suite, Adobe CS

Microsoft Office suite

Photography, CSS, typography, PowerPoint

Experience in the development of visual and graphic images and audio logos, business cards Word Press

Ability to present vague information in a clear and transparent manner to the customer

A basic understanding of programming languages and coding such as HTML, C++ basic concepts of Java can the value of your business more effectively.

Branding ability

Minimum of three years experience

After demonstrating your outstanding abilities, you work in persuading your client declaring your passion and commitment to the task. Make sure that your client believes that you're worthy of the task and are ready to impress them with your imagination and creative capacity. Don't forget to attach the documents of your previous work as proof of your excellent and appreciated expectations to former clients. Don't begin to discuss any personal information that's not professional since there is no chance to present your own personal perspective on your life to clients. Make sure your overview is simple and includes certain keywords that are professionally as it ought to be. Once you've figured out what you should write and what you should not include in your overview, let's take a an overview of two examples of the overviews for profile pages for graphic designers.

Sample 01: Overview of the Upwork Profile for Graphic Designers

Hello!

I'm graphic designer for the three years. I possess a vast knowledge of creating audio, graphics or visual illustrations for illustration of products as well as logos and websites. I am enthusiastic and passionate to design and possess the ability to design extraordinary designs that have a high impact on the eye in accordance with the requirements and demands of the clients.

In addition, I possess the knowledge of the ever-changing business environment. I also think up new ideas and can create new concepts, designs and layouts that are suited to client's needs that be different from other designs. I am extremely knowledgeable of images, colors, font style and layout and I can design designs for small and large corporations, and even individuals.

Chapter 8: Freelance Sites Like Upwork (Best Alternatives)

The growing number of searches for "freelance websites" as well as "online working websites" proves that freelance jobs are getting more sought-after every day. The platform for freelancers is expanding rapidly to keep up with the work and job market. Upwork is now one of the largest and most viewed websites for freelance jobs worldwide. People often search for sites like Upwork due to the fact that they don't like working on the site or being suspended. In the end, competition on upwork is increasing each day. Check out: Upwork or Freelancer, which is superior.

Particularly, being freelancers has become extremely well-liked by those who enjoy the freedom such independent jobs give. Upwork is a company that offers freelance work. has a total of 09 million freelancers registered and 1.5 million customers. But what are other freelancing sites that are popular and which make finding jobs simpler? This is the list of Top 33 freelancing websites that are highly regarded by freelancers.

01. Fiverr

Global Alexa Rank: 333

The thing that most freelancers aren't aware of is that Fiverr is the largest marketplace online for freelance services , which is more extensive than any other market in the world. The name Fiverr is derived from the initial launch with a price of $5 for each job that was completed. In February of 2010 the first meeting of Fiverr was located in Israel and its current headquarters is in Tel Aviv. Fiverr was established in the year 2000 by Shai Wininger, and Micha Kaufman.

It is among the most popular freelancing websites that are utilized by freelancers who offer services to clients around the world. In 2012, it offered a total of 3 million of services. It also offers services for use in English, Spanish, French, Dutch and Portuguese. For a freelancer to work on Fiverr it is necessary to sign up for a fast and easy registration is required , as do most of the most popular marketplaces for freelance work have.

02. Upwork

Global Alexa Rank: 679

It was initially called the Elance-oDesk at its early days. It's a global freelancing platform that lets millions of contractors and freelancers come together and collaborate from a distance to ensure a successful project.

The current location is California, United States. Stratis Karamanlakis, along with Odysseas Tsatalos are the founders of the company. Elance-oDesk changed its name to Upwork in the year 2015. Since then, Stephane Kasriel has been acting as the company's CEO. The company has 9 million freelancers who are registered as freelancers, and 4 million clients registered.

On Upwork, you will find 3 million job listings that are worth $1 billion a year. They believe that due to their simple and reliable marketing practices, this figure will increase by a factor of double or even triple of the current number.

03. Freelancer

Global Alexa Rank: 787

Freelancer is one of the biggest crowdsourcing marketplaces on the world of web. Customers can post jobs on the site and freelancers can submit bids against them and be hired. It's similar to Upwork.

Freelancer.com is so well-known that in some instances it is even more popular than Upwork itself! It's certainly not absurd when you consider that the site has more than 15 million members registered who have shared greater than 7.4 millions of projects. The price of the projects, as a whole exceeds $2.2 billion dollars annually.

Freelancer has worked in partnership with their various subsidiaries such as Freelancer.com, Escrow.com, Warrior Forum, SydStart, Freelancer Technology Pty Limited and numerous others.

04. 99designs

Global Alexa Rank: 3,529

It is essentially an online design competition site. In contrast to other marketplaces for freelancing This site specifically offers freelance design and decorating.

A majority of their clients come from small-sized businesses as well as interior decoration business owners. People of all classes and preference visit this site to purchase graphic designs such as corporate logos and business cards websites, t-shirts and many more.

The thing that is interesting about 99designs is that it's a platform where designers from around the world compete with fellow designers in design contests in order for prizes. They also develop their skills, and develop relations with potential clients. This is fascinating for freelance designers.

Perhaps this is the only site where, if clients aren't pleased with the designs they submit to contests, they give a 100 percent refund assurance. Matt Mickiewicz is the Founder of 99Designs along with two other companies called Sitepoint as well as Flippa.

05. Toptal

Global Alexa Rank: 5,464

Toptal offers an America located Freelance marketplace, online outsourcing site , and Employment website that gives freelance software engineers as well as designers and finance experts to businesses. Simply put, Toptal works like a tool that will bring you to your ideal or desired work.

How Toptal can actually do is after having read your CV or resume they will suggest that you apply to various businesses based on your skills. Toptal is the only freelance marketplace that has gained recognition for being a totally virtual company since all their operations are carried out the internet, with no physical office space.

It was founded in the year 2010 in Silicon Valley, California, U.S by two of its key participants, Taso Du Val and BreandenBeneschott. Taso Du Val is the founder and has been its CEO from then until the present day.

Toptal has been named the No.1 fastest-growing talent market within North America by several consulting firms. Example: In November 2015, Toptal was ranked first by the consultant firm Deloitte.

06. Simply Employed

Global Alexa Rank: 4,353

Simply Hired isn't just an employment site, but also a mobile app as well as an online recruitment advertisement network. The principal job of the business is to collect jobs from thousands of websites on the Web including job boards, newspapers and classified listings, organizations social networks, news sites , and career websites for companies.

After acquiring the job listings, it posts the jobs to its mobile application, website and blogs, social networks as well as other web partners.

Job seekers who sign up on Simply Hired can browse for job openings by keyword or the location of their choice to locate jobs that are of interest. Simply Hired currently operates their job search engines across 24 other countries.

GautamGodhwani together With Anil Godhwani, Peter Weck invested $1.2M USD in 2003 to launch the business. Then, their three distinct series C, D and E have raised USD $13.5 millions, $4.6 million as well as $12 million cash.

07. Guru

Global Alexa Rank: 6,524

Guru.com is a kind of agency-based business. There are thousands of freelancers. Companies are able to find their names, employ their services and earn commissions. Their headquarters are at the same location since the start of its existence. The name of the creator is InderGuglani. The company was established in 2002 through Unicru located in Portland.

08. FlexJobs

Global Alexa Rank: 7,091

FlexJobs is among the most reputable and committed marketplaces that is at the very top list of those looking for flexibility when it comes to their job since they are focused on working at home.

The cost for a subscription to the website will be $14.95 per month, however there are options for annual or three-month memberships. There is a money-back assurance if you alter your subscription so that it will end after a month. The company was founded around 2007 by Sara Sutton is its current CEO.

09. Remote

Global Alexa Rank: 50,589

It is a great platform for remote workers as well as clients. It functions as a connector agency and receive commissions. They've connected 2 million freelancers and clients who have remote work.

The site makes use of various machines learning and artificial intelligence techniques to analyze the skills, experience and personality traits to identify the most likely chance of success in a job. So, the recruiter understands the risk and the likelihood of his investment.

10. OnlineJobs

Global Alexa Rank: 33,320

OnlineJobs is an online Filipino job site that provides exclusive remote job opportunities for workers from all over the globe. It was established in 2009 by the Utah-based Entrepreneur Jonas.

Jonas is also the name of Jonas Replace Myself which is another well-known freelancing site for education. The filtering feature of OnlineJobs is truly amazing, where you can filter it according to ability, level or date.

Toptal vs. Upwork World's Best Comparison

Toptal vs . Upwork: Which is better? Find the most effective freelance marketplace has become a crucial concern for new freelancers and their clients. Topal as well as Upwork both are among the most well-known freelancing platforms in the world. But which is the most effective between upwork and toptal?

This most comprehensive comparison of Toptal and Upwork will help you aware of which one to pick. Two different platforms doing the same job. Both have advantages and disadvantages, however it is the case that you don't know the strengths and weaknesses of each one.

Let's take a look at the differences between Toptal and Upwork as it's a good idea to look at the different platforms available prior to choosing the best one. There is also Upwork and Freelancer

Toptal vs. Upwork Foundation

Topal Upwork

Toptal is the name given to it. Toptal is a result from "Top talent". Toptal is a private business in

America established in 2010 by Tsa Du Val (CEO) and Breanden Beneschott in the year 2010. The company was founded within Silicon Valley, Californiaa, U.S. Although it was initially created as a platform for freelancers for software engineers currently, it functions to be an Industry of Freelance Marketplace, Online Outsourcing and Employment Website. Toptal is a company owned by Toptal is owned with the help of Andreessen Horowitz, Adam D'Angelo along with Ryan Rockefeller. However, Upwork was established in the year 2015. The full name of the company will be Upwork Global Inc. It is actually joined with the earlier ElanceOdesk. Odesk on December 18, 2013. You should be aware that Elance was established in 1999 and has the result that Upwork could be considered to be the most established industry in the marketplaces for freelance. It was founded by a group of people in Mountain View, California and committed to serving the world.

Let's examine the overall contrast among Toptal with Upwork in a tabulated format. It will assist you to know the key aspects.

Toptal vs. Upwork: At A Glance

Subjects Upwork Toptal

1. The Year of the Founded, 2015

2. Established by the founders of Mountain View, California Silicon Valley, Californiaa, U.S

3. It was founded by a merger that consists of Odesk as well as Elance Taso Du Val, Breanden Beneschot

4. 100% Customer Satisfaction 100 100%

5. Rated Score 9.7 9.3

6. Pricing $500 $60

7. The Scheme of Price Quote Based and no-cost Quote Based and one-time payment

8. Approve all freelancers of any ability, but only to the most highly skilled freelancer

9. Famous Clients AirBnb, Instapage, Dropbox Boulder, CSR Limited University of Colorado, Bridgestone

10. Application Devices Windows, Linux, Android, iPhone, iPad, Mac web-based Windows, Mac, Web-based

11. Language English English

12. Test of freelancers, Non-Compulsory

Okay, if you would like to know how the score is overall and satisfaction of users, then we'll say "Rating: 9.7" of Upwork's score, while their overall ranking for Toptal has "Rating: 9.3". Both of their users satisfaction scores are 100%..

Approval of Profile

Toptal Upwork

Toptal is a company that only hires the top talent such as top software engineers and designers, among others. They do not hire everyone who is just applying for freelancing with them. Instead, they only accept three percent of applicants. As an hiring manager, if would prefer to avoid a massive market and select several, then Toptal will be the best choice for you. If you are a first-time freelancer, who wants to join Toptal you'll need to complete four crucial steps in order before you can be accepted into Toptal. These are:

1. Vocal interview to test for language

2. Skills reviews to test abilities and the knowledge gained

3. Live tests are used to demonstrate one's abilities and

4. Finally , practice the project in order to evaluate the project from a global perspective. However, since it is a combined company that includes previous Odesk as well as Elance, Upwork covers a huge platform. It is home to a huge number of freelancers with all kinds of qualifications and all costs. In the end, you have the opportunity to pick from a vast pool of. It's not only for experienced developers but it is open to all types of talents, resulting in an extensive platform for freelancers. It is a means of connecting thousands of freelancers with millions of customers with a one profile every.

Therefore, if you're not an expert and don't have the ability to gain approval from Toptal. This is an unnecessary waste of time. Better to go with Freelancer or Upwork.

Cost of joining

It's a crucial comparison among all freelancing platforms. However, Upwork is completely free for joining. You can join at any time without any payment for joining. However, Toptal doesn't offer full opportunities to sign up. You be able to pay fees for joining to join Toptal.

Toptal vs. Upwork: About the Vendors

Toptal Upwork

We've already mentioned that Toptal restricts its freelancers and clients with diverse terms and conditions. There are more than 2000 clients that work with Toptal. In addition, thousands of designers and developers are employed with us from 93 countries. Toptal has set up strict and obligatory tests for applicants to ensure that they are most skilled and proficient freelancers. The tests test technical abilities, communication abilities, level of experience and test projects, among others. However, Upwork arranges a huge marketplace that aims to become the largest global freelance talent market. It's fast and growing rapidly, expanding quickly across all parts of the world. It is available to anyone regardless of their level of experience and is free to join. Freelancers earn around $1.5 billion annually on upwork.

Upwork compares to Toptal Toptal and Upwork are the most well-known clients:

The most prominent clients of Toptal include Bridgestone, University of Colorado, Boulder, CSR Limited. While Upwork is home to the most prominent clients: Instapage, AieBnB, Dropbox.